TRANSF...

BROCK...

HIGH SCHOOL

HIGH STANDARDS, HIGH EXPECTATIONS, NO EXCUSES

Susan Szachowicz

Copyright © 2013 by International Center for Leadership in Education, Inc.
All rights reserved.
Published by International Center for Leadership in Education, Inc.
Printed in the U.S.A.

ISBN-13: 978-1-938925-21-4
ISBN-10: 1-938925-22-X

International Center for Leadership in Education, Inc.
1587 Route 146
Rexford, New York 12148
(518) 399-2776
fax (518) 399-7607
www.LeaderEd.com
info@LeaderEd.com

Dedication

As a Brockton kid myself, I dedicate this book to all Brockton High students past and present. Thank you for inspiring me, teaching me, and making me smile every day. Thanks to you I had the best job in the world. You are the real champions of this story. *Go Boxers!*

> *A portion of the proceeds from the sale of this book will be donated to the Boxer Champion Fund to benefit Brockton High School.*

Contents

Acknowledgments

My deepest appreciation is for all those who have made this "against all odds" story happen. Brockton High School is an amazing place filled with so many committed people determined to help our students become successful, happy, and the best they can be. It was truly an honor and a privilege to spend my entire career in "Boxer Country." There are some special people in our story to whom I am indebted.

Paul Laurino, my original co-chair of the Restructuring Committee, my colleague, and my friend. You always maintained an unwavering belief in the potential of urban kids. And no matter how tough the day was, you always made me laugh. Still do!

Maria LeFort, my first Associate Principal for Curriculum and Instruction. Professionally, you always exemplified the meaning of instructional leadership, and personally, you gave me loyalty, support, and forever friendship.

Sharon Wolder, my Associate Principal for Curriculum and Instruction, an incredible leader and one of the finest teachers ever. You push our kids, challenge them, set the bar high, support them, and never give up on them. Brockton High is so fortunate to have you, and I cherish our friendship.

Vincent Macrina, our music director, my friend. Through your example you taught us all about the power of music and the arts in our pursuit of literacy. Your insistence on working hard, following your passion, and being the best you can be inspired us all. Thank you, "Bruce."

It takes a team, and Brockton High has the best. Our Administrative Team is second to none. Thank you for insisting on high expectations for our students, our faculty, and ourselves, and for taking such good care of Brockton's kids.

I am grateful for all of my colleagues and friends who stepped up to lead as part of our Restructuring Committee over the years. Although there are too many to name individually, every single member helped transform Brockton High, and it took courage to step up.

I was privileged to work with a faculty that made Brockton High a School of Champions. They believe that every student *can* and *must* succeed, and were willing to do whatever it takes to ensure the success of every student.

Bill Daggett, the Founder and Chairman of the International Center for Leadership in Education, I admire your leadership in education; you have always put the children first. Your recognition of Brockton High as a Model School inspired us to go even further. I continue to learn from you. You have assembled an amazing team of professionals, and I am grateful to the entire ICLE team.

Ray McNulty, you are a champion for all kids. I love our brainstorming, planning, collaborating, our friendship; you challenge my thinking. And as we solve the problems of the world, we always end up laughing.

So many friends and colleagues have provided support and encouragement and urged me to finally write "the Brockton Story." Thank you for pushing me. And to all those who shared the Brockton High story publicly or in the media, thank you for your confidence in us. Your positive words encouraged us to keep pushing harder.

My parents, Eddie and Louise Quagge, instilled in me the values that shaped me as an educator; I miss them deeply. My sister Maureen, a wonderful elementary reading teacher, has brought the joy of reading to thousands of children. And Kristi and Kylie, my special nieces, I always thought about both of you whenever I had to make decisions that affected children.

Finally, my heart belongs to one of Brockton's finest teachers ever—and the best partner anyone could ever have—Bill Szachowicz. His students were lucky to have him as a teacher, but I am the luckiest—he is my husband. I love you.

Foreword

The numbers are remarkable: 4,300 students in one high school, 72% free and reduced lunch, 74% minority, 58% first language not English—yet one of the highest performing high schools in the state of Massachusetts with 25% of graduates receiving state scholarships.

While these numbers are impressive, the story behind these numbers is even more impressive and provides great insight into Brockton High School's extraordinary success.

Sue Szachowicz and her colleagues at Brockton High School built a culture of respect and responsibility for their students and, in turn, earned the respect of the students. That culture is immediately evident through the staff, students, and even the physical building itself. I believe it is that culture that provided the foundation that ultimately has led to great academic success.

As we at the International Center for Leadership in Education studied the nation's most rapidly improving schools in a joint five-year study with the Council of Chief State School Officers, we found that these schools did not just focus on academics. To summarize their focus we created the Learning Criteria comprised of:

- **Foundation Learning:** Achievement in the core subjects of English language arts, math, science, and others identified by the school
- **Stretch Learning:** Demonstration of rigorous and relevant learning beyond minimum requirements, such as participation and achievement in higher-level courses and specialized courses
- **Learner Engagement:** The extent to which students are motivated and committed to learning, have a sense of belonging and accomplishment, and have relationships with adults, peers, and parents that support learning
- **Personal Skill Development:** Measures of personal, social, service, and leadership skills and demonstrations of positive behaviors and attitudes

For Brockton and the nation's most rapidly improving schools, school improvement efforts operate in reverse order of the four criteria listed above. By focusing on Personal Skills Development and Learner Engagement, they create the culture that enables Foundation Learning and Stretch Learning to succeed.

The following are two examples of the Personal Skill Development culture spontaneously played out in Brockton.

- Brockton is near Boston. Shortly after the Boston Marathon bombing, Caris Martinez, a Brockton High School senior, approached the associate principal and said, "We have to show support for the victims." She and other students designed a T-shirt that said "Boston Strong." Selling the shirts, students raised $7,500 for The One Fund Boston in the first day.
- The same week as the Boston Marathon bombing, Brockton High School had their junior prom. Diane Davis, chairperson of the special education department, wrote this e-mail to the class of 2014 after the prom. The groups she refers to (Green House, Azure, Red House, Yellow) are the student cohorts within the high school.

Dear Class of 2014:

After the last few weeks of struggling with feelings of hopelessness and helplessness, you reminded me that there is much more kindness and goodness in the world than darkness and bad. On Friday night at your prom, you demonstrated acts of kindness toward a classmate that he will remember forever. It started when he attempted to navigate the tables and chairs using his walker. As I began to move the chairs quickly, Kelsey Lima from the Green House stepped in and started moving chairs ahead of him. She then invited him to sit at her table to be closer to the dance floor. Keila Andrade from Azure welcomed him into her group of friends taking over the dance floor. Imagine his delight as the entire dance floor surrounded him and cheered for him as he danced. Then it was time to hit the photo booth. He waited in line for a long time when Red House student Adam Cormier and his date took silly group photos with him. Finally, Salea Gonsalves from Yellow topped off the night by encircling his waist and supporting him so he could dance without his walker for a brief time. There were others who made this night memorable for him and, for you all, I am truly grateful. Brockton High is a model school; not just for its academic achievements but also for its truly inclusive environment. As we greeted his mom after the dance, I encouraged him: "Tell her who the star of the prom was!" With a giant, beaming smile he replied, "I was." You are truly a class with class.

Brockton High School is not just a story of great academic success. It is a story of enabling every child to become all they are capable of being—academically, socially, and civilly.

To Sue Szachowicz and her colleagues, thank you for the tens of thousands of students you have made so successful. Thank you for being a model school for all of us to learn from. Thank you for preparing your students to help keep America great!

Bill Daggett, Ed.D.
Founder and Chairman
International Center for Leadership in Education

Introduction

The Journey Begins

"Is this the best we can be?" Teachers and administrators at Brockton High School were forced to ask this question when we received the dismal results from the 1998 Massachusetts Comprehensive Assessment System (MCAS), the Commonwealth's high-stakes test. Brockton High School was then ranked as one of the lowest-scoring schools in the state with a 44% failure rate in English/ Language Arts and a 75% failure rate in math. Because students in Massachusetts had to pass the MCAS in ELA and math to earn a diploma beginning with MCAS 2001, hundreds of Brockton High School students were at risk of not graduating from high school.

Yet despite the massive failure, nothing changed at Brockton High. Another year of testing arrived, and the students were no better prepared for the challenge. In 1999 the failure rate in ELA remained nearly the same (41%), and the math failure rate actually worsened (77%). Perhaps the most depressing day came on December 8, 1999, when Brockton High found itself highlighted on the front page of the *Boston Globe* as one of the worst schools in Massachusetts. We could not deny it; we were in trouble.

MCAS Results 1999					
English			Math		
District	1999	1998	District	1999	1998
Holyoke	40	40	Seven Hills	79	62
Springfield	34	29	Holyoke	77	83
Seven Hills	33	23	Lawrence	76	75
Lawrence	32	33	Springfield	74	72
Chelsea	29	26	Lynn	71	69
Lynn	29	27	New Bedford	68	64
New Bedford	28	25	Brockton	66	68
Fitchburg	27	24	Sabis International	66	45
Worcester	27	23	Fall River	65	73
Boston	26	29	Lowell	65	70
Lowell	26	30	Renaissance	65	91
Fall River	24	24	Chelsea	64	63
Greenfield	23	20	Fitchburg	63	60
Brockton	22	21	Palmer	63	56
Webster	22	17	Chicopee	60	60
Renaissance	21	34	Revere	60	63
Haverhill	20	16	Taunton	60	63
North Adams	20	19	Boston	59	68
Revere	20	14	Everett	59	49
Taunton	19	24	North Adams	58	60

Data from Massachusetts Department of Elementary and Secondary Education

Fast forward a decade. On October 9, 2009, we were back on the front page of the *Boston Globe*, but this time the headline read, "Turn Around at Brockton High." Our school had outperformed over 90% of Massachusetts high schools. On January 14, 2010, we were featured in *Education Week's Quality Counts* edition for our students' academic performance on the state assessments. Later that year, Brockton High was featured in the report *How High Schools Become Exemplary* (http://www.agi.harvard.edu/events/2009Conference/2009AGIReport.php), published by Harvard economist Ronald F. Ferguson, who researched the minority achievement gap. Perhaps the most incredible moment came on September 28, 2010: Brockton High was featured on the front page of the *New York Times* for outstanding student achievement. For each of the past ten years, we have proudly announced to our school community that we have been selected by the International Center for Leadership in Education to be a National Model School.

The last decade has been one of improvement, student achievement, success, and accolades. How did this happen? This is the story of the turnaround of Brockton High School.

The purpose of this book is twofold. The first is to experience the journey of transformation at Brockton High School. Although external forces of educational reform laws and regulations prompted this turnaround, the efforts of the team within the school brought about the dramatic change and have sustained the academic improvement for over a decade. This change was no fluke or one-time spike in students' scores; this was a true culture change in a large, complex, traditional urban high school.

The second purpose is to provide a template for replicating this type of literacy initiative in your own school. When we present the story of Brockton High School, we are often asked if this initiative is sustainable and replicable. The answer is an emphatic "Yes!" to both questions. Our students have demonstrated consistent, sustained improvement for over a decade. The initiative is also replicable because it is about a process, rather than any person or program. Hundreds of educators from schools and districts across the country have visited Brockton High over the past ten years, and many have adopted and adapted our Literacy Initiative to fit their students' needs. Just ask Principal Ron Rix from

South Middle School in Westfield, Massachusetts. Ron visited Brockton High with a team of teachers from his middle school, and they rolled up their sleeves and began their own literacy initiative. The results at South Middle School tell the story. Their school made AYP and has been selected by the International Center for Leadership in Education to be a National Model School.

We have included many of our model Literacy Workshops and training scripts at the end of this book. Our hope is that you will use these to guide your own process of change. They are intended to be adjusted, adapted, and revised to fit your needs. We hope that you find them helpful and informative.

CHAPTER ONE

The Brockton Story

The City and Its High School

Called the "City of Champions" in honor of world champion boxers Rocky "The Brockton Blockbuster" Marciano and "Marvelous" Marvin Hagler, the city of Brockton is located approximately 25 miles south of Boston.

Photo: Bill Szachowicz

Brockton is a large urban center with a population of approximately 95,000 residents whose median income is well below the state average. Once a leader in the shoe manufacturing industry, Brockton experienced a decline in shoe factories throughout the 1990s, causing the city to struggle economically. As the shoe factories that provided employment for this immigrant city closed down, no industrial base replaced those jobs, and unemployment soared. Housing foreclosures resulted in the city being littered with abandoned properties. Crime and homelessness spiked.

Despite the city's economic decline, Brockton High School remained a source of pride. The city celebrated the athletic accomplishments and performing arts programs of its high school. No doubt that it had much to celebrate. The athletic trophy cases were filled with football championship trophies, and the gym walls were covered with athletic banners announcing the championships of the many athletic teams in the school. Marciano Stadium was filled with fans for Friday night football games, and the gym was often loud with pride during basketball season.

In addition, Brocktonians supported the strong arts programs and flocked to our concerts and drama productions. Our students' artwork was displayed throughout the city. The walls and trophy cases in our Fine Arts Building were adorned with student work, as well as plaques and trophies announcing state and national awards. These programs in athletics and the arts were an important part of the life and spirit of the school; they provided important learning experiences for all students, kept many students engaged with school, and connected the school to the community. However, they were not the principle measure of the school's condition. Unfortunately in 1998, the city's pride in the athletic and arts programs at Brockton High could not be extended to the academic performance of the school.

Brockton High School Then

For decades the school leadership had a philosophy that educational programs were available for the students, and students needed to take advantage of them. In fact, the principal at the time often stated, "A student has a right to fail," and teachers were told to allow students to sleep in class if that was what students wished to do. Many students in classrooms and in the cafeterias slouched with their heads down, even sound asleep. If a teacher asked students to pick their heads up, the most common response was, "I have a right to fail." And fail they did— in large numbers.

Many faculty and administrators did not believe the students could succeed academically. When in 1998 the Commonwealth of Massachusetts instituted the high-stakes testing program (MCAS), one administrator stood in front of Brockton High faculty and stated that the tests were much too hard for Brockton High students; he was sure that most of the students would no longer earn a diploma. Because he believed so few would graduate, he even cynically commented that we would have to move our graduation out of the football stadium and into the school's Little Theater.

Traditional in its organization, Brockton High had very specific content area departments, which presented another challenge. Students on the MCAS were tested in English and math, and teachers in the other content area disciplines did not feel any ownership for the students' performance. When the initial test results were announced to the faculty, teachers could be heard saying, "I'm glad I don't teach English or math."

Given the "right to fail" attitude prevalent in the school, not surprisingly the first round of results from the MCAS ranked Brockton High School as one of the lowest scoring schools in the state. Brockton High was mired in low expectations, excuse making, and a leadership unwilling to look inward to make change.

Brockton High School Now

Boston Globe reporter James Vaznis began his article on the turnaround at Brockton High with the following paragraph:

> BROCKTON—Brockton High School has every excuse for failure, serving a city plagued by crime, poverty, housing foreclosures, and homelessness. Almost two-

thirds of the students qualify for free or reduced-price lunches, and 14% are learning to speak English. More than two-thirds are African-American or Latino—groups that have lagged behind their peers across the state on standardized tests. But Brockton High, by far the state's largest public high school with 4,200 students, has found a success in recent years that has eluded many of the state's urban schools: MCAS scores are soaring, earning the school state recognition as a symbol of urban hope.

While Brockton High may have used every excuse for failure in the past, we accept no excuses for failure now. Yes, we face many challenges, but our message is strong: High Standards, High Expectations, No Excuses.

Our Students

Brockton High is the largest high school in the Commonwealth of Massachusetts, and with 4,200 students in grades 9–12, it is one of the largest high schools in the country. The student population is diverse racially, ethnically, and socioeconomically. Fifty-nine percent of the students are black, which includes African-Americans, Cape Verdeans, Haitians, and many students from the Caribbean. Twenty-four percent are white, and 12% are Hispanic. Over one-third of the students at Brockton High are Cape Verdean, a country off the west coast of Africa. Seventeen percent are classified as Limited English Proficient, and over 40% do not speak English as their first language. Over the past five years in Brockton the bilingual population of students has tripled. Seventy-six percent of the students live in poverty and receive free or reduced-price lunch. The Massachusetts Department of Elementary and Secondary Education classifies 79.2% of our students as "High Needs." Many of our students are the first in their families to graduate from high school, and most are first in their families to attend college.

Brockton High School Demographics
• Comprehensive High School Grades 9–12
• Enrollment: 4,181 students
• Poverty Level: 76%
• Minority Population: 76%
• 50 different languages
• 40% speak another language in the home
• Approximately 17% in Transitional Bilingual Education
• Approximately 11% receive Special Education Services

Brockton High School Students
• 59% Black: includes African American, Cape Verdean, Haitian, Jamaican, and others
• 24% White
• 12% Hispanic
• 2.7% Asian

Our Faculty and Administration

The dramatic, substantive changes at Brockton High have taken hard work, a tenacious focus on improving student academic achievement, and an unwillingness to give up on any student. Long gone are the days of the administration predicting that our students will not pass the MCAS and lamenting that the test is too hard, too long, and certainly too challenging for our students. Now Brockton High is a school all about the academic success of every student; faculty eagerly awaits MCAS scores and takes pride in the success of each student. The faculty feel totally invested in their students' success.

Brockton High has 334 faculty members representing a myriad of departments, with each department supervised by a department head who teaches a reduced schedule. The "big four" content area departments are English, Math, Science, and Social Science. The Department of Special Education and the Department of Bilingual Education are also large departments that support our students with disabilities and our English language learners. The other departments are Foreign Language; Business, Career, and Technology; Music; Art; Wellness; JROTC; Project Grads (a program for parenting teens); and Guidance. Approximately 85 members of our faculty are Brockton High alumni who have returned to teach.

The Administrative Team works collaboratively to ensure the smooth operation of the school and the delivery of quality instruction to the students. Brockton High has four color-coded houses (Red, Green, Azure, and Yellow) to which students are assigned for their four years. Leading the Administrative Team are the Principal and Associate Principal for Curriculum and Instruction. Each of the color-coded houses has a Housemaster, essentially a principal of one house consisting of approximately one thousand students, and an Assistant Housemaster. These House teams deal with the day-to-day issues that arise in the school.

Schedule and Requirements

The Brockton High schedule is a modified block design. Students take five classes in the course of the day; each period is between 66 and 70 minutes in length. Major subjects like English and math run as full-year classes that meet daily. Other classes are only a semester in length, and others may meet on an every-other-day schedule. The design of the schedule is complicated but provides students with the opportunity to select from many electives.

Brockton High School Daily Schedule	
Registration Room	7:20–7:25 (5 minutes)
Period 1	7:29–8:38 (69 minutes)
Period 2	8:42–9:48 (66 minutes)
Period 3	9:52–10:58 (66 minutes)

Period 4	Students are assigned to one of the following:
	• **Student A:** With Lunch 1, L2-L3 class
	  ○ Lunch L1: 11:02 – 11:35 (33 minutes)
	  ○ Class L2-L3: 11:39 – 12:49 (70 minutes)
	• **Student B:** With Lunch 2, L1-L3 class (70 minutes total for class)
	  ○ Class L1: 11:02–11:39 (37 minutes) (NOTE: Students MUST STAY IN CLASS until the 11:39 time tone; they MUST NOT MOVE at the 11:35 time tone!)
	  ○ Lunch L2: 11:42–12:12 (30 minutes)
	  ○ Class L3: 12:16–12:49 (33 minutes)
	• **Student C:** With Lunch 3, L1-L2 class
	  ○ Class L1-L2: 11:02–12:12 (70 minutes)
	  ○ Lunch L3: 12:16–12:49 (33 minutes)

Period 5	12:53–1:59 (66 minutes)

Students must meet local graduation requirements which include successfully completing four years of English, three years of math, three years of science, three years of social science, and a number of credits in the electives. As required by the Commonwealth of Massachusetts, every student must pass the MCAS in English/Language Arts, math, and science to earn a diploma. If students meet local graduation requirements but do not pass the MCAS, the state mandates that they receive a Certificate of Attainments in place of a diploma. There are no exceptions to the MCAS requirement.

Throughout the four years of study, guidance staff and teachers advise and consult with students. Students are encouraged early to identify career plans and aspirations. Students establish an educational plan outlining high school courses, extracurricular activities, and community service that will assist them to reach their goals. Despite our large student population, strong relationships among and between the faculty, administration, students, and parents have been essential to our students' success.

While this chapter has provided an overview of Brockton High School, the story of the turnaround begins with the implementation of the Literacy Initiative that will be detailed in the following chapters. The shaping of Brockton High School's present philosophy—*High Standards, High Expectations, No Excuses*—and the schoolwide focus on literacy can be traced to a number of factors. The state educational reforms, particularly the implementation of the MCAS requirement for graduation, provided the impetus for the change process. While the mandates from the state motivated the change, the faculty and administration stepped forward to lead the change process at Brockton High School. The changes have been substantive, significant, and focused on student achievement from high-quality instruction and assessment. Continuously examining data and adjusting and improving practices have dramatically improved student achievement and ensured success for every student. Most importantly, the changes have provided Brockton's students with opportunities to earn their diploma, go to college, and achieve their goals.

The next chapters describe how Brockton High School transformed from a designated failing school to one ranked by the Massachusetts Department of Education as a Level One School (www.doe.mass.edu/apa/ayp/2012/levels.xlsx), receiving both state and national honors and awards. There is no silver bullet or magic secret. This story is one of hard work and tenacity based on four major steps:

1. Empower a team.
2. Focus on literacy with NO exceptions.
3. Implement with fidelity according to a detailed plan.
4. Monitor extensively.

The following chapters specify these steps so that every school can adapt the process used at Brockton High to implement a schoolwide literacy initiative. The chapters also tell the story of how Brockton High has evolved, and continues to evolve, from a traditional high school celebrating athletics and performing arts to one celebrating the academic achievements of students. The story is truly a narrative of change—continuous change. Perhaps the most significant change of all has come with a belief in the possibilities, opportunities, and positive spirit that these changes can bring about in the school. After spending a day at Brockton High, the Massachusetts Commissioner of Elementary and Secondary Education, Mitchell Chester, told the *Boston Globe*, "To me, Brockton High is evidence that schools that serve diverse populations can be high-achieving schools. It's just very graphically ingrained in my mind after having walked through the building and gone into classes that there's a culture of respect among students and adults. You don't see that in every school."

The belief that improvement is continuous and never ending is not just the vision of a leader or a small group of teachers; it is now the culture of the entire school. We are far from finished. Brockton High School is an institution that has spent almost a decade combining its best traditions with literacy essential for our students' lives beyond high school. While we have accomplished much, not all is complete. Until every student in the school graduates at the proficient level—ready and able to reach his or her highest goal—we have more improvements to make. We will continue to examine data, target, respond, develop a plan, implement, monitor, assess effectiveness, and revise if necessary. While we are a school still very proud of our athletic and performing arts accomplishments, we are even prouder of our academic successes and now celebrate those enthusiastically. Brockton High School remains a work in progress and continues to champion our *High Standards, High Expectations, No Excuses* philosophy.

Chapter Two

How Did We Begin?

The demands of the Massachusetts Educational Reform Law of 1993 should have signaled to all schools that the status quo was no longer acceptable. This complex and comprehensive law changed education in the state by establishing new time and learning requirements, calling for the development of state curriculum standards, and mandating the Massachusetts Comprehensive Assessment System (MCAS). The MCAS included a high stakes assessment at the high school level. Schools across Massachusetts now had to meet the demands of this educational reform legislation.

Despite the very clear provisions of this law, the prevailing attitude in many schools in Massachusetts was denial. The state has a strong local control tradition, and the thought that Massachusetts would deny a diploma to a student based upon test results was not only unheard of in the state but also unbelievable. Frankly, Brockton High was in that category of schools denying that anything would change. Rather than examining the curriculum, aligning it to the new state standards, and reviewing the sample assessments provided by the state, Brockton High did not change course. The MCAS results clearly demonstrated that.

Facing the Failure

In 1998 our students sat for the MCAS for the first time. Needless to say, they were woefully unprepared. As shown in the performance chart, 44% of Brockton High's students failed English, and 75% failed math in the first round of testing. Even with results as shocking as these, the school did not enact serious changes.

MCAS: Grade 10 English Language Arts
Percentage of Students by Performance Level

Performance Category	1998	1999	2000
Advanced	2	2	6
Proficient	20	22	21
Needs Improvement	34	35	32
Failing	44	41	41

Massachusetts Department of Elementary and Secondary Education

MCAS: Grade 10 Math
Percentage of Students by Performance Level

Performance Category	1998	1999	2000
Advanced	1	2	5
Proficient	6	7	11
Needs Improvement	17	16	21
Failing	75	76	64

Massachusetts Department of Elementary and Secondary Education

The next year brought another round of MCAS and significant failure for Brockton High students. The faculty gathered in a meeting in the auditorium to hear the results: 41% of our students failed ELA, and the math results worsened from the year before with 76% of students now failing. However, even with such dismal results a second year in a row, Brockton High did not focus on changing the way it was educating its students.

Instead, the denial comments dominated. "There will be a lawsuit by parents that will stop the MCAS!" declared one teacher. Another said, "If the students aren't going to take their education seriously, there's nothing I can do about it." "I'm sure glad I don't teach English or math" was a common refrain. The faculty as a whole had no sense of ownership over student performance.

The public became aware of the failure on December 8, 1999 when Brockton High was highlighted by the *Boston Globe* as one of the worst schools in Massachusetts. The article described the large numbers of students at Brockton High and other failing schools who would not earn a diploma because of their MCAS failure.

The faculty meeting following the *Globe* article did change the dialogue among many: "Is there something we can do? We have to try something" was heard more often. The principal, who had been appointed in 1998, was frustrated by the lack of improvement among the students and brought in a couple of department heads to brainstorm ideas. At Brockton High, department heads are the leaders of a specific content area department; they teach a reduced class load and supervise the teachers in their department. During that brainstorming session, the two department heads suggested that they convene a group of faculty and administrators to tackle the MCAS issue and the myriad problems with student academic achievement. This was the genesis of Brockton High School's turnaround.

It Began With a Team

The first order of business for this twosome was recruitment, and given the negative attitude prevalent among so many of the faculty, this was not an easy task. Both department heads recognized that including every department and recruiting a balance of administrators and teachers was very important. They sent out notices requesting participation but received minimal response. Trying a more aggressive recruitment, they sought out faculty members they saw as leaders and in some cases begged them to participate. The department heads' persistence paid off. While not every department was represented, they were able to recruit 20 members to their new committee.

Thanks to the support of the Superintendent of Schools, members of this new committee were paid according to the hourly rate established by the contract. Funding for the Restructuring Committee was critical: the school system needed to show the value of this leadership group and the importance of its work. In addition, the Brockton superintendent set aside a portion of the professional development monies for the district in a fund called Challenge for Change. Principals were invited to apply for Challenge for Change funding to support a school improvement proposal. This financial support for positive change signaled its importance. This funding continues today.

When this new committee came together for the initial meeting on a Saturday morning, it was co-chaired by the two department heads. The first order of business was to name itself, and the second was to establish its clear mission. After a lively discussion, the group settled on the Restructuring Committee as its name to reflect the significant change that needed to take place at Brockton High. From the outset, this group did not aim solely at improving MCAS scores. Rather, the objective was to improve the academic achievement of all students. The Restructuring Committee unanimously agreed on the slogan *High Standards, High Expectations, No Excuses*.

Next the group developed a mission and set of ground rules: *Keep it simple* became the maxim. The group swiftly agreed on the mission:

1. Improve students' academic achievement
2. Personalize the educational experience for every student

The MCAS indicated that we had to improve the academic performance of our students. With over 4,000 students in Brockton High, the group also determined that it was too easy for students to disappear, remain silent, and feel disengaged. The members strongly believed that personalizing students' experiences at school was essential for their success. These two goals remain the centerpiece of the Restructuring Committee because they focus on continuous improvement.

Establishing the ground rules was also a fairly easy process. The committee quickly agreed on three ground rules. First, a respectful dialogue was essential. Second, criticizing someone else's suggestion or idea had to be accompanied by a suggestion; decrying an idea by saying it just would not work was unacceptable. The third and final rule concerned using discretion when it came to the committee's conversations. The group often threw out suggestions and worked through brainstorming ideas during this process. If members of the Restructuring Committee had gone into the teachers' rooms and started talking about these ideas, people may have gotten upset unnecessarily. Also, sharing discussions and ideas could have undermined the process of open and free discussion and violated members' trust. When the Restructuring Committee was ready to go ahead with a plan, the group shared key information with faculty and led discussions and training sessions. However, until the group decided to initiate a carefully devised and detailed plan, members of the committee agreed to keep the discussions within the Restructuring room.

After establishing these rules, the group created a calendar of meetings, with each meeting having a clear agenda. Members determined that the committee would meet monthly at a minimum and more frequently as necessary. To ensure intense, focused, and productive meetings, the group met Saturday mornings from eight until noon, avoiding some of the challenges of after-school meetings. However, timelines sometimes necessitated additional meetings after school. Once the mission, ground rules, and procedures were established, the group was ready to examine data.

Data, Data, Data

To develop an agenda for the significant change process, the committee explored information present in the field. Rather than basing change on merely anecdotal information or local institutional critiques, the group utilized a variety of data to review its expectations for student learning and to reflect on its ability to address student needs, community expectations, and state standards. This data included national documents, which gave voice to universal educational initiatives, existing successes, and data beyond local results. *Shopping Mall High School* by A. G. Powell and D. K. Cohen was essential in articulating how America's high schools were broad in offerings but shallow in focus. *Breaking Ranks: Changing an American Institution,* a report by the National Association of Secondary School Principals, outlined the need for risk and creativity in designing the contemporary high school. *Who Moved My Cheese?* by Johnson Spencer, M.D. and Kenneth Blanchard articulated the reasons for opposition to change, the fears that change generates, and the ways change can be accomplished. All of these documents provided committee members a variety of important perspectives.

Having studied and planned our approach by examining these national documents, the Restructuring Committee began to examine specific data related to Brockton High, particularly the MCAS results. While we knew the abysmal failure rate, we really didn't know much beyond the numbers.

The committee started by reviewing the actual released test questions from the first two years of the test. In the Restructuring work room, members spread out the test questions and started reading and reviewing. After an hour everyone reconvened and shared their impressions. Our conclusions from that first review of the MCAS and our subsequent plan taught us a hard lesson.

Lesson Learned the Hard Way

When the Restructuring Committee gathered to share impressions of the first two years of the MCAS test, the group initially focused on the content of the test questions. In particular, we noticed a large number of questions about Shakespeare on the ELA test: students had to read numerous excerpts from Shakespearean plays and a few sonnets. In response to this content, the committee sought to launch a Brockton High Shakespearean experience.

The few English teachers on the Restructuring Committee excitedly began to suggest a course of action that involved focusing on Shakespeare in every English class. MCAS testing would begin in late April. The committee planned for the grand Shakespearean learning experience to take place throughout March and April. During these two months students all over Brockton High acted out scenes from Shakespearean plays and analyzed sonnets; however, they were not happy. Despite the students' response, the committee preserved the thought that if we could meet this Shakespearean challenge, the scores would go up.

While the Committee believed that our actions would better prepare students for the MCAS, we were soon disappointed. Imagine our distress when our students opened their test booklets that year and saw not one question about Shakespeare.

After much venting in the next Restructuring Committee meeting, the group realized an important lesson, one we were glad to learn early in our transformation: we could never outguess a test, and no school improvement plan should focus on a test. Our path to improvement could not be about what the test makers might ask in any particular year. Rather, our path had to focus on what students needed to know and do to be successful, not only in their academic careers but in their lives long after school. In other words, the group needed to focus its efforts in a completely different direction. In addition, the committee concluded that helping students acquire those skills was the responsibility of every teacher in the school, not just of one department. While the path to improvement hit a snag with the Great Shakespearean Fiasco, the lesson moved us from simply reacting to a test to focusing on best practices for engaging and empowering students.

Back to the Data

After the Great Shakespearean Fiasco, the MCAS scores barely budged for the third year in a row. Not surprisingly, the 2000 results were depressing: the English Language Arts failure rate decreased only three percentage points to 41%, and the math failure rate was still an alarming 64%.

The Restructuring Committee scheduled two meetings during the summer of 2000 to evaluate its strategy. We again reviewed the test questions, but this time we asked a different question: What skills and knowledge did our students need to know and demonstrate to be successful on the test? This question brought different answers than our first approach. We noticed that students had to read many difficult, complex passages and write responses to those reading passages. We also noticed that they had to solve many complex problems with multiple parts. The MCAS test was rigorous.

The Committee also reviewed Brockton High's schoolwide item analysis. The students were scoring well below the state average on every writing question, and over half of the questions on the test required writing. Even many math questions asked students to explain their answers. While many questions required writing, numerous students were leaving the writing portions blank, not even attempting to answer them.

The group's analysis of the data also showed that students were not prepared for the complex problem solving and critical thinking that was required of them. Furthermore, after breaking down the subgroups included in the MCAS report, the Committee concluded that our failure was not limited to any one group of students; it was schoolwide. The message was clear: implementing a test prep program would not be enough. We needed to address the standards and instruction across the school.

After developing a list of skills and knowledge that students needed to demonstrate on the MCAS, the Committee broadened its discussion and focused on the skills and knowledge required to graduate and be successful in life beyond Brockton High School. The list was enlightening. Members prioritized skills such as speaking in complete sentences, presenting information effectively, and solving problems in the workplace. These were not skills taught in textbooks.

While developing the list of skills and competencies was straightforward and fairly easy, the discussion that followed was far more difficult. Evaluating our own practices regarding the rigor of our standards and the quality and consistency of instruction across the school led to some concerning observations. The Restructuring Committee began to ask some important questions.

- What are we teaching?
- How are we teaching it?
- How do we know the students are learning it?

- We are not likely to get any additional staffing or resources, so what resources do we have now that we can use more effectively?
- What can we control? What can't we control?
- Is this the BEST we can be?

The last question prompted a resounding "No!" from the Restructuring Committee. However, left unsaid was the understanding that unless we did something differently, this would likely be the best we could be. This change was not about the students: it was about how we taught the students. After tackling these questions, a strategy began to unfold.

This powerful discussion by a group of educators was the impetus for our schoolwide focus on literacy. Reading, writing, speaking, and reasoning became the core values that anchored the discussions and planning in the committee's meetings from that point forward. For students to be successful, every teacher in every department had to be part of this educational shift. This daunting challenge facing the Restructuring Committee was one we were ready to take on.

References

National Association of Secondary School Principals (1996). *Breaking ranks: Changing an American institution.* Reston, VA: National Association of Secondary School Principals.

Powell, A. G., Farrar, E, and Cohen, D. K. (1985). *The shopping mall high school: Winners and losers in the educational marketplace.* Boston: Houghton Mifflin.

Spencer, Johnson and Blanchard, Kenneth (1998). *Who Moved My Cheese?* New York: G. P. Putnam's Sons.

Chapter Three

The Literacy Initiative: Focus, Focus, Focus

Literacy for All, No Exceptions

The Restructuring Committee meetings now had a focus, but also a major challenge. The committee had established two goals: improving student academic achievement and personalizing the educational experience for all students. After the Great Shakespearean Fiasco, the group realized that trying to outguess the MCAS test was not the path to improved student academic performance. Instead, we determined that our focus had to be on literacy. Every teacher in the school needed to be part of literacy instruction. However, what did that mean? While the Restructuring Committee embraced the focus on literacy, we did not have a shared understanding of the term *literacy*. What did literacy mean for our students? Did it mean they could read a newspaper? Did it mean they could read their textbook or perhaps read at grade level? Did it mean they could solve problems? Our next step was to create a common definition of *literacy*.

How We Defined Literacy

This series of Restructuring Committee meetings were some of the most exciting but also some of the most frustrating. A real think tank in action, members pulled ideas from many different places to develop the definition of *literacy*. Despite the variety of ideas, the group agreed that literacy encompassed much more than reading and writing: it involved critical thinking and problem solving. To detail more specific literacy skills, the Restructuring Committee divided into four groups: Reading, Writing, Speaking, and Critical Thinking. Each group worked to articulate the specific skills and competencies that students needed in these four literacy areas.

The subcommittees drafted their lists of skills and then reconvened with the committee to share their suggestions. Members reviewed, argued, and revised. Discussions were spirited, exciting, and always focused on what was best for the students. The group's goal was to develop a list that was comprehensive but also simply stated using the following criteria:

- The literacy objective had to be stated clearly so that anyone—student, parent, teacher, community member—would understand the skill.
- The literacy objective had to be interdisciplinary, something applicable in every class and subject.
- The literacy objective had to be applicable for *all* students, including gifted and talented students and students with disabilities.

The Restructuring Committee made two important decisions in its first review. We changed *critical thinking* to *reasoning* because the word seemed more active, more interdisciplinary, and more encompassing of math and science. In addition, after a spirited debate about listening, we decided not to use a listening category. One faculty member on the committee made that case passionately by stating, "Students are already doing too much listening around here. We need to get away from the teacher talk and make the students become active learners. If we include listening as one of our central literacy areas, too many teachers will say that they are working on students' listening skills and continue the lecture approach." The powerful comment brought all committee members to agree on four skill areas for the Literacy Initiative: Reading, Writing, Speaking, and Reasoning.

After two meetings of thoughtful deliberations, the Committee found real value in its progress. One member said, "I think we're really on to something. If we could get every student in the school to learn how to do all of these skills, students would be ready for MCAS, and they would be successful in all of their classes." The Literacy Initiative began to take shape.

The Restructuring Committee wanted to visually represent these skills and decided on four charts—the Literacy Charts. Each chart listed a series of specific skills regarding reading, writing, speaking, or reasoning and could be posted in every classroom in the school. These visuals symbolically reflected the link of literacy to all subject areas. In addition, each chart included the definition of *literacy* for Brockton High School.

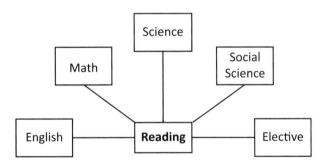

- for content (both literal and inferential)
- to apply pre-reading, during reading, and post-reading strategies to all reading assignments, including determining purpose and pre-learning vocabulary
- to research a topic
- to gather information
- to comprehend an argument
- to determine the main idea of a passage
- to understand a concept and construct meaning
- to expand one's experiences

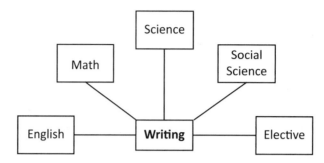

- to take notes
- to explain one's thinking
- to argue a thesis and support one's thinking
- to compare and contrast
- to write an open response
- to describe an experiment, report one's findings, and report one's conclusions
- to generate a response to what one has heard, viewed, or read
- to convey one's thinking in complete sentences
- to develop an expository essay with a formal structure

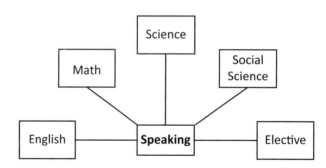

- to convey one's thinking in complete sentences
- to interpret a passage orally
- to debate an issue
- to participate in class discussion or a public forum
- to make an oral presentation to one's class, one's peers, one's community
- to present one's portfolio
- to respond to what one has read, viewed, or heard
- to communicate in a manner that allows one to be both heard and understood

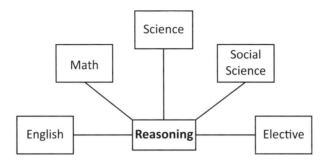

- to create, interpret, and explain a table, chart, or graph
- to compute, interpret, and explain numbers
- to read, break down, and solve a word problem
- to interpret and present statistics that support an argument or hypothesis
- to identify a pattern, explain a pattern, and/or make a prediction based on a pattern
- to detect the fallacy in an argument or a proof
- to explain the logic of an argument or solution
- to use analogies and/or evidence to support one's thinking
- to explain and/or interpret relationships of space and time

How We Engaged the Faculty

As excited as the committee was for the key literacy skills to provide an academic focus for the school, the excitement was at this time confined to the members of the Restructuring Committee. Even though members had worked diligently on the Literacy Initiative, we were only 22 teachers and administrators out of a faculty and administration of 334. Our next challenge was to share these skills and engage faculty in the development of a schoolwide Literacy Initiative.

Realizing that the schoolwide Literacy Initiative would likely meet tremendous resistance, the Committee spent many hours planning how to involve the faculty. Ensuring that the faculty had a strong voice in the development and implementation was critical.

Since Brockton had a strong teachers' union and a very structured contract, the Restructuring Committee could not call faculty meetings whenever we wanted. As per the teachers' contract, two designated faculty meetings took place each month, with each meeting lasting only one hour after the end of the contractual student day. Traditionally one meeting was used for administrative announcements; it was often cancelled and rarely had an agenda. The second meeting in the month was designated as a department meeting run by the content area department head. Committee members knew that we needed that meeting time to get faculty input on the Literacy Initiative. The co-chairs met with the principal, explained the proposed Literacy Initiative, and requested that the Restructuring Committee be allowed to plan the faculty meetings for the next two or three months. As the principal was facing tremendous pressure to improve students' MCAS scores, he was supportive of the plan.

With a meeting time planned, the Restructuring Committee needed a thoughtful strategy to introduce the Literacy Initiative. The committee required a focused agenda to maximize the 45 minutes of work time available at each meeting.

Keeping the faculty discussion groups interdisciplinary was the committee's first important decision about how to structure the meetings. Brockton High was traditional in its design, and teachers identified themselves by content area. In fact, because the faculty was so large, many teachers in different disciplines did not even know each other. The committee wanted to break down those content walls so that everyone focused on literacy rather than subject. This key decision propelled the Literacy Initiative forward.

The Restructuring Committee began by dividing the faculty into interdisciplinary discussion groups of 12–15 teachers; each discussion group was facilitated by a member of the committee. Every teacher was provided with the drafts of the four Literacy Charts. At the top of the charts we put the students' MCAS scores (41% failed English and 76% failed math) with this question: Is this the BEST we can be? The facilitators had an outline for navigating their discussion group using the following two agenda items.

1. Explain why we are focusing on the MCAS scores and asking, "Is this the BEST we can be?" During this agenda item, facilitators reminded everyone that school improvement was not only about MCAS but also about helping students improve their

academic performance and preparing them for lives beyond
Brockton High School.

2. Explain the goal for the meeting: review and help revise the
drafts of the Literacy Charts. Facilitators did this by discussing
three questions during the meeting:

   a. In each of the four areas (Reading, Writing, Speaking, and
   Reasoning), have we included what is required for our
   students to be successful in your class/your content area?
   What skills and competencies are missing?

   b. Is the literacy skill stated clearly so that all teachers and
   students can understand it? If not, how should we phrase it?

   c. Literacy should not only be the domain of English classes.
   Students should be demonstrating these skills and
   expressing themselves well in every classroom. Is the skill
   applicable to your content area? To all content areas? When
   you read these skills, do you find yourself saying, "Yes, a
   student should be able to do this in my class"? If not, how
   should we rephrase these skills? Should any be deleted?

After each interdisciplinary faculty discussion on the proposed
Literacy Charts, the Restructuring Committee debriefed. We put all of
the faculty recommendations on the table to determine what needed
to be revised and how to make changes. Then we brought the revised
Literacy Charts to the next interdisciplinary discussion group meeting.
The drafts of these charts went out to the faculty four or five times
before the committee settled on the final version.

The Literacy Charts represented a significant intellectual change
within the institution. They defined the school's academic expectations
for student learning in specific, measurable ways and gave Brockton
High a schoolwide focus for the first time. Certain reading, writing,
speaking, and critical thinking skills—long viewed as the responsibility
of a few departments—now were the responsibility of all teachers
and departments, challenging the traditional segregation of content
areas in the high school setting. Those challenges began as these
interdisciplinary discussion groups proceeded.

Faculty Buy-In

When the Restructuring Committee started this process, we did not have faculty buy-in. However, if the committee had waited for that buy-in to occur, we would very likely still be waiting today. What we did have was widespread failure on a high-stakes state exam and a need to do something fast. Students' diplomas were on the line.

During the interdisciplinary faculty discussions, the negativity was sometimes overwhelming, particularly for Restructuring Committee members who were facilitating the discussion groups. Facilitators heard many of the same comments: "I was hired to teach art. I am *not* a reading teacher." "What can we expect from students with their backgrounds?" "I am a scientist, not an English teacher." "Yet another plan. Don't worry; it won't last." After each one of these interdisciplinary discussion group meetings, the Restructuring Committee debriefed. Some committee members expressed frustration at the negativity of so many members of the faculty. They felt that their discussion groups were not moving forward because one or two negative faculty voices dominated their groups.

At that point a couple of committee members devised a clever strategy to minimize the negative voices. During Restructuring Committee debriefings, the same faculty names surfaced as being particularly cantankerous and disagreeable. Because these negative voices dominated and often intimidated colleagues, thereby stifling productive discussions, the committee tried grouping faculty members differently. When making the discussion group assignments, the committee put all of the notoriously negative people in the same groups. This strategy changed the entire process because now the other groups could move their discussions forward. All faculty members, no matter what group they were assigned to, still had the opportunity to voice their concerns and offer their suggestions, opinions, and ideas. After the committee implemented this new approach, meetings became more productive and the Literacy Initiative moved forward.

Engaging the Parents and the Community

While the interdisciplinary faculty discussions were proceeding, the Restructuring Committee also sent home copies of the Literacy Charts along with an explanation of the Literacy Initiative and invited parents to comment. During our scheduled meetings with parents throughout the year, we presented the Literacy Charts and invited comments. Also, the co-chairs of the Restructuring Committee, along with a few members of the committee, conducted evening meetings with parents and community members to get their input. We also organized a small group of Brockton business leaders to share our work with them and seek their suggestions about skills they felt the students needed for the workplace. The suggestions and revisions of the parents and community were shared with the faculty, and many were incorporated into the final copy of the Literacy Charts. The Restructuring Committee felt great pride when the Chairman of Brockton's Chamber of Commerce spoke publicly at one of these meetings and stated, "These literacy skills are excellent, and they go beyond school. These skills represent what our employees need. If you could get Brockton High students to demonstrate these skills, they would be ready for anything." That was a powerful moment for all of us on the Restructuring Committee.

Key to the transformation of Brockton High School was the tenacity of the Restructuring Committee. They listened to the skepticism of the faculty, responded to faculty concerns, and preserved the strength to stay the course. In every discussion group, the Restructuring facilitator presented the student achievement statistics and reminded all participants of the essential question: "Is this the best we can be?"

The Restructuring Committee learned from experience that true buy-in comes only with positive results—our greatest test. Now that the Literacy Charts were developed, the committee had three big challenges: how to bring the Literacy Charts to life, how to have everyone teach the literacy objectives to the students, and how to assess students' mastery of these skills.

Chapter Four

The Key to Success: Adult Learning

The process of creating our Literacy Charts took the better part of a year. The Restructuring Committee shared the charts with faculty multiple times for their comments, suggestions, and revisions until we agreed on the final list of literacy skills. The faculty rooms were buzzing. Some comments were positive. "This is the first time I ever remember being asked what I thought was important," one veteran teacher shared at a meeting. Many were negative. "I hope that the Restructuring Committee doesn't expect us to do something with these lists. Who do they think they are?" Most comments expressed faculty concerns about what was next; "So now what?" and "What am I expected to do with this?" were frequently asked questions.

"Now what?" was the most important question that the Restructuring Committee had to answer. Our many years in education taught us that while we could have many three-ring binders of creative ideas, they might never come off the shelves. Simply having lists of literacy skills was not enough to improve students' academic performance.

The Restructuring Committee talked at length about how these literacy skills could become a common vocabulary in the school. One of our members said, "We all know these skills and own them. How can we get that same ownership to spread to the faculty?" The discussion centered on visually displaying these literacy skills using Reading,

Writing, Speaking, and Reasoning as the centerpiece of each chart. The content area departments would then surround the literacy skill.

This design led to an important decision by the Restructuring Committee. We agreed to produce these charts professionally on large posters and have them prominently displayed in every classroom and office so that teachers and students could easily read them. Our graphics department developed a brochure about the school that highlighted the Literacy Charts, and we sent the brochure to the parents and the city's businesses and agencies. The public presentation of the Literacy Charts elevated the importance of these documents and confirmed our commitment to use the Literacy Initiative as the mission of the school. All of the skills and competencies detailed in the Literacy Charts now had to become part of the ongoing, everyday life of the school.

Training for Every Teacher

One thing was clear—simply posting Literacy Charts on the classroom walls was not enough. Bringing the Literacy Initiative to life at Brockton High required a change in instruction. Teachers needed to learn how to teach and integrate these skills in their classes. With so many skills detailed in the Literacy Charts, the challenge was where to begin. Faculty and students would be overwhelmed if we tried to incorporate too many skills at once.

The Restructuring Committee went back to the data to determine where to start, and Brockton High's MCAS data was revealing. Brockton High's students had failed in large numbers; however, a closer look at the item analysis showed that students were significantly below the state average in every open-response question on both the English Language Arts exam and the math exam. In ELA, the open-response questions required students to read complex passages from literature or lengthy nonfiction pieces and then answer a question about that reading in essay form. In math, open-response questions required students to solve multistep, complex problems and explain their answers. The data revealed that not only were our students below the state average on open-response items, but often they were leaving the items blank. With over half of the MCAS points from writing, this needed to be our focus.

While the Restructuring Committee used data from the MCAS test to draw conclusions, we learned from the Great Shakespearean Fiasco that trying to outguess a test was not going to improve our students' skills. The Restructuring Committee had a spirited discussion about which of the literacy skills best crossed disciplinary lines to help teachers understand the value of the skill for learning material in their content area. All committee members agreed that writing needed to be the target skill. As one of the committee members said enthusiastically, "Writing is thinking. If students can articulate their thoughts clearly in writing, we can better assess their mastery of the skill and their mastery of our subject area." With universal agreement, the Restructuring Committee determined that writing was the place to start.

Just as we had to define what we meant by *literacy* at Brockton High, so we also had to define the steps in our open-response writing process. We wanted to develop a process that was simple, clear, and easily implemented in every subject area by every teacher. We needed a schoolwide definition of what *open-response writing* meant and a schoolwide, step-by-step open-response writing process.

Brockton High School: Open Response Steps to Follow

A small group of our Restructuring Committee developed the workshop. They drafted a 10-step writing process that every student would follow.

1. Read question carefully.
2. Circle or underline key words.
3. Restate question as thesis (leaving blanks).
4. Read passage carefully.
5. Take notes that respond to the question.
    Brainstorm and map out your answer.
6. Complete your thesis.
7. Write your response carefully, using your map as a guide.
8. Strategically repeat key words from your thesis in your body and in your end sentence.
9. Paragraph your response.
10. Reread and edit your response.

More importantly, the group drafted a process for teaching the open-response writing process that every teacher would follow. They brought all of the Restructuring Committee together to test this process for our first Literacy Workshop. Essentially the committee had three responsibilities. First, we had to go through the Open-Response Writing Literacy Workshop as learners. Second, we had to be thoughtful critics of the workshop: What were the strong points? What needed clarification? What needed to be revised? What needed to be omitted? Third, we had to figure out how to present this workshop to the faculty. A key component of our Literacy Initiative was a train-the-trainer approach: we developed the workshop and then trained ourselves to deliver it to our colleagues. We were the learners, the critics, and the future trainers.

As the Restructuring Committee went through the Open-Response Writing Workshop, we became excited about this schoolwide approach to writing and convinced of its potential to make a difference for our students. The subcommittee took our critiques and made revisions. Soon we were ready to roll out our first Literacy Workshop to the entire faculty.

The plan was to teach the open-response writing process to all teachers, who would then teach it to all students using their content area as the context for reading and writing. Open-response writing was the first of our Literacy Workshops and evolved into the centerpiece of our transformation. (See Chapter Eight for the script used for the Open-Response Writing Workshop.)

Now that the first Literacy Workshop was ready, the co-chairs of the Restructuring Committee met with the principal to share the design of the workshop and make a request. The committee needed the next two faculty meetings to train all of the teachers. Since meetings were limited to two per month and no meeting could extend beyond one hour after the regular student dismissal time, we had to plan the workshop carefully. The principal agreed to give the committee both meetings to prepare everyone appropriately. He was highly supportive of the Literacy Workshop on open-response writing, and we were ready to proceed.

The first Literacy Workshop was interdisciplinary, so that the focus was on the literacy skill—open-response writing—rather than on any subject matter. Teachers were assigned to interdisciplinary groups of approximately 15–20 members. The committee chose readings from the previously released MCAS exams hoping that teachers would gain familiarity with the rigor of the MCAS exam while learning how to teach the open-response writing process.

During the follow-up workshop, which occurred two weeks later, teachers reviewed the open-response writing training in their content area departments. The department heads chose readings appropriate to the subject matter. The Restructuring Committee felt that the two sessions reinforced the open-response writing steps, modeled the teaching process, and demonstrated how it related to every content discipline.

Scripting to Ensure Consistency

To ensure that Restructuring Committee members consistently delivered the Open-Response Writing Literacy Workshop, we wrote a detailed training script. The script also modeled how faculty should teach open-response writing to their students. The agenda for the one-hour interactive presentation defined what open-response writing was, taught every teacher the step-by-step process to instruct their students, and provided a rubric for teachers to assess students' open-response writing. (See page 95 for full teacher training materials.)

The key to success was not so much the specific open-response writing steps but rather the consistency by which they were applied schoolwide. Literacy Workshop: Teaching Open-Response Writing presented ten steps that every teacher would now teach to students; the workshop truly modeled best practices. Every teacher in every discipline would now teach students how to write open responses and assess those responses using the same process and rubric. After these two sessions on open-response writing, the schoolwide Literacy Initiative was ready to begin.

Highly Structured Implementation: We All Do It "This Way"

Beginning the Literacy Initiative with the open-response writing was not an accident. At one of the Restructuring Committee meetings, members had a frank discussion about the importance of a structured implementation. Most were frustrated with previous professional development sessions that lacked follow-up. Our experience taught us that without a highly structured implementation plan, some teachers would immediately and frequently use the open-response writing format, others would use it once or twice, and many would never use it. We needed universal compliance for our schoolwide Literacy Initiative to be effective.

However, devising a plan for over 300 teachers presented a formidable challenge, and the committee struggled with how to do this. The breakthrough came when our discussion shifted from what teachers had to do to what students needed to do. In order for students to master open-response writing, they needed repeated practice over time. The Restructuring Committee discussed a plan to provide students with repeated opportunities to learn and practice this writing skill.

The committee proposed a calendar for implementation that was supported enthusiastically by the administration; this schedule benefited students and allowed for close administrative oversight. Specifically, the committee assigned each department a week during which every teacher in that department taught the open-response writing lesson using the appropriate content for that day. Using this prescribed calendar allowed students to practice this literacy skill every few weeks throughout the year. Practice was key to student mastery of the literacy skill.

Sample Open Response Calendar of Implementation Memo
The Open Response calendar of implementation is as follows:

1. November 2–6:   Social Science, Social Science Bilingual
2. November 30–   Wellness, JROTC
   December 4:
3. December 14–18: Science, Science Bilingual
4. January 11–15:   Business, Technology, and Career Education
5. January 25–29:   Math, Math Bilingual
6. February 22–26:   Foreign Language, Special Education
7. March 7–11:   English, ESL, Guidance
8. March 20–24:   Family and Consumer Science, Project Grads
9. April 5–9:   Music, Art

As a follow up to this activity, department heads are required to collect from each teacher at least one student sample from each of the teacher's classes. The student samples should include:

- Student name
- Teacher name
- Date
- Course name and level
- Period
- A copy of the reading selection and question
- Evidence of the student's active reading
- All prewriting work that the student did; e.g. webs
- A copy of the written open response
- The new scoring rubric and completed assessment

After you have collected the samples from each teacher and reviewed them for quality and completeness, please send them to me in a department folder with a checklist of your teachers. Please be sure that your teachers clearly label their student samples.

Thank you for your help and your support with this important endeavor. Your work contributes directly to the improvement of our students in this critical area. Your continued support and the efforts of your faculty are essential to the success of our students, and we thank you.

Prior to sending out the calendar of implementation, the co-chairs of the Restructuring Committee and the principal met with the president of the teachers' union and the union's leadership team to ensure that union grievances would not derail implementation. While the committee knew that we had not violated the contract, the meeting was still positive for both sides. By communicating with the union and potentially gaining their support, we hoped to avoid the lengthy and often frustrating grievance process.

After a lengthy meeting during which the entire Literacy Initiative—training, implementation, and monitoring—was discussed, the union leadership expressed cautious support for the plan. They indicated that they had received many calls from their membership expressing concern about the Literacy Initiative; however, they felt that teachers had been trained appropriately, were given clear notice and planning time, were provided with a rubric to assess the writing, and most importantly, had nothing in their contract being violated by the Literacy Initiative. The union knew that they would benefit if the Literacy Initiative worked and student performance improved. The students' success would be a direct result of the instruction they received, and that would reflect well on the teachers' union.

Now that the training of all faculty and administration was complete, we had the enthusiastic support of the school and central office administration, and the teachers' union cautiously supported our plan, we were ready for actual implementation.

The Writing Begins

Because we are a traditional high school with content-specific disciplines, we organized the implementation according to subject area. The Social Science department was the first to teach the open-response writing. During the first week of November, every Social Science teacher taught the open-response lesson using whatever content was being taught that week. For example, if I were planning to teach about the Revolutionary War, I would select a challenging reading about the Revolutionary War and create an open-response question about that particular reading. I would then teach the students the ten-step open-response writing process and model that process for them, sharing the rubric with the students prior to writing. An important component of the writing process was sharing the assessment criteria in advance so the students were informed of the standards by which they would be evaluated. After teachers completed the open-response writing lesson during their assigned week, they assessed the students' writing using the rubric and then turned the students' work in to their department heads for review.

The Restructuring Committee deliberately selected the Social Science department to kick off the process. A few members of the Social Science department were on the Restructuring Committee, and they were strong teacher leaders who were very positive about this initiative. They felt they could promote a positive tone about this writing initiative with their colleagues, and we hoped that the initial open-response writing would be handled in a positive, productive way by the faculty. Also one of the co-chairs of the Restructuring Committee was the Social Science department head, so the committee had strong administrative support within that department. In addition, the Social Science department often incorporated challenging primary source documents, so open-response writing was a good fit.

That strategy seemed prudent. After the teachers' open-response week concluded, the comments among the Social Science department faculty were encouraging. Comments such as "That wasn't bad at all," "The students seemed to get it," and "I think it really went well" were common. The buzz in the faculty room was relatively positive. Our decision to use the Social Science department first seemed to pay off.

A couple of weeks later, the Wellness department and the JROTC program were scheduled to begin. The committee wanted to engage the electives right away, and the department heads in both of these areas were very supportive. However, the Wellness department asked for more support from the Restructuring Committee in finding appropriate readings and creating rigorous open-ended questions. A few members of the Restructuring Committee worked with the Wellness department for a couple of weeks prior to their implementation to ensure that the teachers felt prepared and comfortable with the material.

Every two to three weeks the students were challenged in one of their classes with open-response writing as established by the calendar of implementation. The class had a clear structure. The teacher began the class by explaining the Literacy Initiative and why we were doing this. Next they modeled for the students the open-response writing process and then provided guided practice on the ten steps. Teachers introduced the rubric that would be used to assess students' writing. Following the guided practice, students independently practiced the ten steps. Students completed an open-response writing exercise on the reading the teacher provided.

This process was repeated in every class that students had over the course of the year. We maintained a tenacious, unwavering focus in implementing this process in every classroom with no exceptions: same objective, same process, same assessment. The students started to recognize that something different was happening in the school—they had never seen such a focus on writing, and they were learning how to write. The key to our success was not the students: the key was the adults. When we started doing things differently, the students started doing better.

Much of the teacher feedback was positive, but as you would expect in such a large faculty, considerable resistance existed. In some cases teachers showed outright defiance. The committee addressed this issue by monitoring the process. Just as we had carefully planned the Literacy Workshop on Open-Response Writing by scripting the training, so we also had planned how to monitor the initiative. Ensuring the rigor and consistency of the open-response writing initiative was critical. Our experience in education had taught us that what gets monitored is what gets done. How we planned, organized, and implemented our monitoring process was crucial to the success of the Literacy Initiative.

Chapter Five

What Gets Monitored Is What Gets Done

The format for implementing the schoolwide, open-response writing initiative was highly structured and methodical. As detailed in the previous chapter, the Restructuring Committee targeted writing as the first literacy skill based on the data and then developed the training script. The committee employed a train-the-trainer approach to instruct all faculty members how to teach the specific writing skill by modeling the process. After training, the committee prescribed a calendar of implementation so that every few weeks students received the same literacy lesson using different content. The format of the lesson was the same; only the context was different. Teachers implemented their open-response writing lesson according to the calendar, and no department was exempt.

The Restructuring Committee employed the same level of meticulous planning for the Literacy Initiative monitoring process as it did for implementation process. Members of the Restructuring Committee frequently stated, "What gets monitored is what gets done!" We felt strongly that nothing could be left to chance, and if we were not relentless about insisting that these literacy lessons be taught a particular way, then we would be shortchanging many students. While some teachers might teach the lesson well and often, others would simply go through the motions and not deliver with quality. Still others would decide not to do it at all. Just as we had insisted on a consistency of standards for students, we had to insist on consistent, high-quality instruction. To ensure that quality, we planned to monitor the faculty as they taught the literacy lessons, the students as they learned to demonstrate the literacy skills, and the administration as they led the efforts to monitor the process. Professor Ronald Ferguson, Director of the Achievement Gap Institute at Harvard University, commended our comprehensive monitoring process in his book *How High Schools Become Exemplary*: "As they implemented their plans, these schools carefully monitored both student and teacher work in order to continuously refine their approaches."

While the Restructuring Committee planned and implemented the monitoring process at Brockton High, the superintendent of schools also worked at the district level to provide better supervision and evaluation, particularly in many of the large schools. He recognized that principals were often diverted from an instructional focus when issues in the schools arose, and he wanted an individual who would have instructional leadership as his or her primary focus. The superintendent created the position of Associate Principal for Curriculum and Instruction and appointed the first associate principal at Brockton High because of the high stakes nature of the MCAS. The principal and associate principal worked closely together, and this position provided tremendous support to the principal and administrative team. Because of the Literacy Initiative at Brockton High, the superintendent and the principal believed that one of the co-chairs of the Restructuring Committee would be the best candidate for the newly created associate principal position. When the superintendent and principal made that appointment, they reinforced the school leadership's commitment to the literacy focus.

A Systematic Monitoring of the Instruction

When the Restructuring Committee planned the implementation of the Literacy Initiative, we had a prolonged discussion about what we needed to evaluate specifically. For the students, we knew that we needed to assess their mastery of the skill. For the faculty, we wanted to ensure that the literacy lessons were taught with fidelity, that the assignments were rigorous, that the student feedback was useful, and that the standards were applied consistently. For the administrators, we needed to make certain that they were assisting faculty with the planning of the literacy lesson, observing the process in the classrooms, providing instructional feedback on the lesson, and reviewing the student work for consistency. However, we were also careful to keep members of the Restructuring Committee in supportive roles with their colleagues as opposed to evaluative roles. This was critical to maintaining trust and collegiality among the faculty.

The Restructuring Committee used a standardized rubric for student work to raise the standards and ensure consistency of rigor. The Restructuring Committee drafted a writing rubric as part of the initial open-response training. Prior to the literacy training, the committee asked a number of faculty members to test the draft of that first rubric in their classes and provide valuable feedback. The open-response writing rubric went through a few revisions before it was used by the full faculty. Including the faculty in the development process was important for engagement. See pages 110–112 for the open-response writing rubric.

As part of the open-response writing lesson, the teachers shared the rubric with students prior to writing so they knew precisely what the assessment standards were. After completing the writing assignment according to the open-response format, students often assessed their own work using the rubric. Then the teachers collected the assignments, assessed them using the rubric, and provided feedback to the students.

After teachers had ample time to assess the writing using the rubric, the department head collected the student work to review for consistency. After teachers within a department reviewed the student work with the department head, the department head met with the associate principal to further review the work for consistency and rigor. This process established an important feedback loop for assessing the effectiveness of the literacy lesson.

Central to the success of the Literacy Initiative was the monitoring of the actual literacy instruction. The Restructuring Committee used a number of important strategies to monitor the implementation of this initiative beginning with open-response writing.

The first element used to monitor implementation was the calendar. With a faculty of over 300 teachers, tracking who was using the open-response writing and when would have been impossible without some organization. Implementing the open-response writing according to a calendar allowed the administrative team to focus their observations on one department. The team could review the lesson plans in advance, know precisely the day(s) that a particular teacher was teaching the lesson, and visit that classroom to observe the lesson. The implementation calendar served two important purposes: it provided the students with repeated and deliberate practice of a skill over time and established a framework for the careful monitoring of the instruction.

Another monitoring strategy was administrative review of teachers' lesson plans prior to the literacy lesson. Brockton's teacher contract required teachers to submit lesson plans on a weekly basis, and the implementation calendar informed administrators which department was teaching the open-response writing skill during a particular week. The administrative team reviewed the lesson plans of that particular department to become familiar with the content of the lesson prior to observing the class.

Of course the most informative and effective monitoring of the Literacy Initiative was the administrative team's actual observation of the classes. Every member of the administrative team was involved in the observations and crossed departmental lines. For example, the art department head observed a science class, or the math department head observed a wellness class. This cross-disciplinary approach highlighted how the open-response writing skill was being taught in every class. While the subject-specific topic for the lesson provided the context for teaching the skill, the focus of the observation was on how the students were being taught the literacy skill. Sometimes the observations lasted the entire class; on other occasions the observation was only a walkthrough. In either case, a number of administrative team members were in classrooms during the assigned week.

Following the observations of a department's implementation, the administrative team debriefed and shared observations. The dialogue was frank and informed the team how the implementation was going: What was working well? What needed refinement? What were teachers struggling with? Then the department head provided feedback to the teachers.

Note that the observations were conducted by members of the administrative team, not members of the Restructuring Committee. We did not want members of the Restructuring Committee to be viewed as evaluators. The committee's collegial support during the preparation and training was essential to Brockton's success, and we wanted the committee to preserve the faculty's trust.

That trust factor among the faculty was particularly important as we began to review student work. As the open-response writing initiative continued, faculty and administration collected the students' writing. Comparing student work became the most important factor in assessing the consistency of our standards.

A Protocol for Collecting and Reviewing Student Work

Collecting student work allowed faculty to examine expectations teachers had for their students and assess the consistency with which the faculty were assessing the literacy skills. Teachers initially reviewed student work within their departments so that instructors had the opportunity to compare similar assignments. As more student work was collected over time, interdisciplinary groups of teachers reviewed the work to provide opportunities for colleagues to compare schoolwide standards. These analytical and reflective discussions resulting from the comparison of student work highlighted the inconsistent expectations we had in our school.

When Brockton faculty and administration first began the process of reviewing student work, the Restructuring Committee was unsure about how to structure the discussions. Teachers were looking at student work but did not have a framework to work from. Although the initial discussions were helpful, the committee wanted a more focused comparison of the quality of work in order to foster significant improvement. To help the faculty and to improve student achievement, the committee developed a set of questions as a protocol for the review of student work.

The faculty helped to develop and test the review protocol and immediately the level of analysis and quality of discussion increased. The protocol consisted of the following questions:

- What were the grading criteria?
- Were the standards high enough? (What is good enough?)
- In what ways does this work meet or fail to meet the set standard?
- What do the student responses indicate about the effectiveness of the assignment?
- How might the assignment be improved?
- Did you find evidence of growth over time?
- What did you notice about consistency across classes and departments?

When teachers began reviewing student work through the framework of these questions, the dialogue was enriched. This process also prompted a number of teachers to request a literacy workshop on how to write effective, rigorous question prompts, which the Committee eventually developed.

Support Systems for All: Students, Teachers, and Administrators

This meticulous monitoring process—involving observation of the instruction of the literacy skill and the collection and review of student work—revealed to the committee that while we were doing a good job developing the training scripts and modeling the instruction for the faculty, we needed to provide more support to both the teachers and students.

Students who needed additional support were identified by our monitoring system. The systematic practice of the open-response writing process was paying off; the review of student work demonstrated improvement in the quality of writing as the year continued. Because we were using a schoolwide rubric, teachers were able to immediately identify those students who needed more writing assistance and direction. Many of the teachers provided extra help to their students in free periods or after school; however, the committee wanted to provide more options for students who needed direct instruction and feedback.

Creating our Access Center provided a tutorial center for students throughout the day and after school. In Brockton's teacher contract, teachers are required to have one administrative duty period in their daily schedule, which is often cafeteria duty or hall monitoring. When the Restructuring Committee opened the Access Center, we recruited teachers who were willing to provide tutoring assistance to the students and assigned that as their administrative duty. Teachers who saw one of their students struggling with writing could refer that student to the Access Center where the student would receive additional one-on-one direct instruction. Juniors and seniors were also recruited to serve in the Access Center as peer tutors; they were well trained on the writing process so that their tutoring was consistent with the schoolwide process. In addition to teacher referral, students were encouraged to independently seek assistance in the Access Center during any unassigned period they had or even after school. Initially, teacher referral was the main reason a student reported to the Access Center; however, as word spread among students that this was a positive, safe, and supportive atmosphere to receive assistance, the Access Center became a bustling place.

Another support program for students was our Boxer-2-Boxer mentoring program. With teacher recommendation, seniors were assigned to assist a teacher in his or her freshman classes, serving almost as a teacher aide. No teacher was required to take on a senior as a Boxer mentor; it was always by teacher request. The seniors who participated received a credit for an Independent Study project. These Boxer mentors helped the teacher implement the Literacy Initiative by reinforcing the teacher's instruction and providing feedback to the students. The program was a win-win for students: freshmen received additional targeted instruction in the classroom, and senior mentors felt valued by making a powerful contribution to school improvement. The program was student leadership in action.

Not only did students need support during the implementation of the Literacy Initiative, but the teachers did as well. The Restructuring Committee was asking teachers to do something that many had never done before, and a number of teachers were nervous about taking it on. For most teachers the two training sessions prior to implementing the open-response writing lesson were sufficient. However, some teachers began asking their department heads or members of the Restructuring Committee for additional assistance. For example, many teachers in the physical education department requested some assistance prior to their week of implementation. A small group of Restructuring Committee members made themselves available during their free periods in the day and after school for teachers who wanted to review their planned lessons. This teacher-to-teacher approach was not evaluative in any way; it was positive, productive, and collegial.

Even the administrative team needed support; they were the front line of the monitoring since the Restructuring Committee was not part of the evaluative process. The members of the administration—

the housemasters, the assistant housemasters, and the department heads—were the point people in delivering feedback to the faculty. This feedback process required consistency.

The Restructuring Committee assigned members of the administrative team to each class to observe the implementation of the open-response writing process. The presence of an administrative team member in the classroom reinforced for both the teacher and the students how important this writing process was. Prior to implementation, members of the administrative team met and established observation criteria. Following a department's week of implementation, the administrative team debriefed and refined the criteria for the next round. In this way we were able to provide valuable feedback to the faculty about the process.

These observations or walkthroughs were aimed at watching the instruction of the literacy skill. The union leadership met with the principal to share concerns of some members who felt that they were being evaluated on something they had never done before. To allay those fears, the school administration agreed not to conduct any formal evaluations of a teacher for personnel purposes during his or her initial week of implementing the open-response writing. The administration reassured union leadership that the process—not the individual— was being observed. This decision satisfied the union concern but still ensured the integrity of the process. However, the administration made it very clear to the union leadership that if any teacher did not complete the open-response writing implementation as directed, he or she would be insubordinate, and disciplinary action would result. Teachers had been trained, had received support, and had access to additional teaching assistance in the classroom if they needed it. Participation was not optional, and the union agreed with this. The union president noted that everyone had been appropriately prepared and given ample notice. In addition teachers were using their own subject matter and being offered assistance. The union was supportive of the literacy effort.

As the process continued throughout the year, the administrative team began meeting frequently to discuss the process of implementation. These discussions were led by the associate principal. Some of the members of the administrative team were highly skilled in observation and evaluation; others needed further training and support.

In order to provide consistency in evaluation across the school, every administrator and the entire instructional leadership team was trained in Research for Better Teaching in Observing and Analyzing Teaching techniques (RBT) by Dr. Jon Saphier. In the years before the Literacy Initiative, classroom evaluations at Brockton High were often general and included subjective comments. Administrators provided teachers limited feedback, if any, on improving instructional practices; as long as the class was quiet, the evaluation was essentially deemed a success. After the RBT training, administrators based classroom observations on specific, observable, and measurable criteria. Evidence was documented, and recommendations for improvement were included on evaluation forms and in post conferences. The post-conference dialogue was positive and centered on improving instruction; it was solidly grounded in observable and measurable criteria and evidence. The report of NEASC's Visiting Team for our accreditation in 2003 stated, "The teacher supervision and evaluation process contributes to the improvement of instructional practices. For the most part the Brockton High School faculty has a positive view of the evaluation process, particularly the practice of post-conferencing. This dialogue, centered on teaching and learning, contributes to reflection about instructional practices for improving student learning. This evaluation process is focused on observing and analyzing teaching through the lens of what students demonstrate in the classroom in response to instruction."

Essentially this initiative served to align the process of formal and informal evaluations according to instructional priorities. Consistency was the watchword. The teachers were all trained in using the open-response writing process. Students were taught this process and held to schoolwide standards. Administrators were also trained how to monitor the process. In his study *How High Schools Become Exemplary*, Professor Ron Ferguson stated about Brockton High, "Leadership teams succeeded because they used their positional authority effectively... they built trust...they found ways to remain respectful of peers, even when asking them to improve their performance." The impact of this schoolwide focus was powerful and produced results.

Dealing With the Resistance

Despite the schoolwide implementation, not everyone was on board. As mentioned earlier, if we had waited for buy-in, we would still be waiting; however, the students could not afford such a waiting period. Not long after the implementation began, so did the resistance.

The resistance seemed to manifest itself on two different levels. The first level was reluctance rather than outright resistance, but these reluctant faculty members often complained about the process. The second level was defiance. These faculty members openly expressed their disagreement and tried to convince others to side with them in opposition. In some cases they were openly insubordinate. The administration dealt with these two types of resistors differently.

The reluctant resistors were not defiant or insubordinate, but they grumbled. Restructuring Committee members heard the complaints in the faculty offices. One committee member recounted to the full committee the concerns a group of colleagues had shared with him. They expressed apprehension about losing valuable time teaching their content to complete the open-response writing assignment. These teachers were not defiant or nasty; they just did not believe the Literacy Initiative was worth doing, and they were convinced it would not work.

For this group of resistors, the course of action was twofold. The Restructuring Committee and the administrative team provided support but also stood firm, insisting that the writing assignment would be done: no exceptions, no exclusions. Both the Restructuring Committee and the administrative team used a few common phrases: "We have to do something, 75% failure." "It's worth a try." "We're open to all suggestions. What would you suggest we do to help the students?" When someone resisted, administrators were encouraged to ask, "Help me understand what you are struggling with." In dealing with someone who was arguing that this was too difficult or beyond his or her ability, we would say, "Let me help you," and offer the direct assistance of colleagues. Administrative presence during the implementation process was critical to ensure that even if a teacher did not support this initiative, he or she still taught it.

The second level of resistors was far more difficult to deal with because they were staunchly opposed. They were vocal in their opposition and determined to recruit other resistors. No amount of support or convincing from the Restructuring Committee, other colleagues, or administrators could convert this group. For this defiant group we resorted to direct administrative mandate. We provided the training, offered support and assistance, but made the bottom line clear: this process would be done according to a prescribed schedule, we would watch them implement the open-response writing lesson, and any refusal would be considered insubordination. Administrative follow-up was crucial; in some cases the follow-up resulted in disciplinary action.

One example occurred early on in the preparation for the open-response writing. A member of the administrative team demonstrated the defiance. To prepare the administrative team for the open-response writing initiative, a few members of the Restructuring Committee provided the team with the training that the faculty would receive so that they knew what the faculty would experience. The principal and associate principal asked members of the administrative team to bring a reading selection appropriate to their content area and some possible questions they might use for the open-response writing implementation. The meeting began positively with the first three department heads sharing their materials and developing powerful questions they might use for the students. However, the meeting came to a grinding halt when one department head who was asked to share his reading and writing suggestion said in front of the entire group, "I don't have anything. We don't do things like this in my department." Suddenly everyone else in the room avoided eye contact. It seemed no one was even breathing. Considering this was a member of the administrative team, we were all shocked. It was a showdown moment.

This was not an issue for the members of the Restructuring Committee to handle; this required administrative action. The associate principal was first to respond and said, "Here's what we can do. Go back to your office now, select a reading that would work well for the open-response writing assignment, and return with it. We'll keep going for now. As soon as you get back here, which should take only 10 or

15 minutes, we will come back to you, have you read your selection, and help you develop a powerful question to use." The department head seemed surprised by this response, probably assuming that we would just skip over him and allow him not to participate. Sending him to get a reading immediately delivered a strong message to everyone that *all* meant *all*. The department head then asked incredulously, "Now? You want me to go get something now and come back with it?" The principal said directly and sternly, "Right now." The principal delivered a very clear directive. Failure to comply would clearly have been an act of insubordination.

The department head left, and the meeting continued. After approximately ten minutes the department head did return with a reading, and as promised, the associate principal came right back to him and asked him to share the reading. The rest of the administrative team provided helpful suggestions about possible questions to use for the open-response writing. The meeting concluded without further defiance. However, as the administrative team packed up to leave the meeting, the principal had one more message for the defiant department head. He asked the department head to come into his office to meet with the associate principal and him. During that meeting, the principal and associate principal reiterated that participation was not optional, and as a leader of a department, he needed to model for others what was necessary. Failure to cooperate and participate would be insubordination, and disciplinary action would result. The department head stated he understood the directive.

Another instance of resistance involved a member of the faculty. After training and the distribution of the implementation calendar, word came back to the administration that an art teacher had covered up the literacy charts in his classroom with student artwork. In addition, on the date that he was to teach the open-response writing assignment, he did not do it. This was a fine teacher, well respected by the students and his colleagues. He was fiercely independent and felt that his classroom was his kingdom. However, the Literacy Initiative required that everyone be held accountable and participate. Once some were allowed exceptions, the initiative would be undermined.

The associate principal met directly with this teacher's department head and directed the department head to meet with the teacher and instruct him to remove the artwork from the literacy charts. If the teacher needed additional space to display student work, he could have access to any of the bulletin boards and display cases in the Fine Arts building and the Main Office area. However, we knew that it was not a case of needing wall space. The department head also informed the teacher that he was required to complete the open-response writing assignment on a specifically assigned day and that the department head would be there to observe the process. Also, if the teacher needed assistance, the associate principal would co-teach the lesson with him. The teacher got the message. He was not happy about doing the lesson, but ultimately he taught it well using an excellent reading selection about how artists determine their subjects and create their works of art. We felt strongly: *all* means *all*.

Perhaps the greatest act of resistance was what we now refer to as the Great Book Burning. During that first year of the Literacy Initiative, we implemented the open-response writing process with tenacity. Although we would not receive the results of the MCAS testing until the fall, we were pleased with the efforts of the faculty, and the students appeared to be better prepared. We watched them actively read the questions, map out their answers, and write detailed responses. The Restructuring Committee and the administrative team wanted to thank the faculty for their efforts; many of them were not supportive of this initiative, but they persevered. We decided to give every faculty member a letter of thanks from the principal and associate principal and a book. We purchased for every teacher Cris Tovani's book *I Read It, but I Don't Get It,* an excellent work on adolescent literacy that is filled with practical strategies. We delivered a copy of the book with the thank-you letter inside to every teacher on the last day of school.

When everyone returned from summer vacation, the buzz went through the school about a summer book burning. A number of teachers came to members of the Restructuring Committee and the administrative team to inform us that over the summer a faculty member had hosted a cook out and asked everyone to bring their copy of Tovani's book so that they could have a book-burning party. A number of faculty members participated, but many more teachers were disgusted. The backlash was so strong that many began denying that this had happened, but we knew, unfortunately, it had.

At our first meeting, the Restructuring Committee discussed the book-burning incident and decided that we needed to change our plans for the first full faculty meeting, which occurred a few weeks after the start of the school year. We wanted to make a strong statement to challenge the book burners, so we decided to use a literacy strategy directly from Tovani's book and model it for the faculty. In the memo to the faculty informing them of the agenda for the first meeting, we asked the teachers to bring their Tovani book with them. If someone needed another copy, he or she had to see the principal and associate principal directly. This announcement got everyone's attention and probably sent some faculty members scrambling to order books via priority mail. One of our Restructuring Committee members summed up our action most eloquently when she told a correspondent from PBS a few years after the incident, "Whether you read it, or burned it, you were still trained in the literacy strategies." We stayed the course and directly challenged the resistors.

No one in administration enjoyed these types of confrontations. However, dealing with this type of resistance was essential to the success of our Literacy Initiative. For many years teachers at Brockton High were allowed to opt out of professional development and ignore school initiatives. Now student diplomas were on the line, and our students needed the initiative. One young department head who faced a particularly resistant veteran teacher talked about the struggle: "It was a battle, and a lot of the conversations were not fun and made my stomach turn. But you just had to plow ahead because we knew it was good for the kids. We saw that literacy was working." The teachers were the key to the students' success. As we taught students differently and prepared them well, they began to do better. Perhaps Harvard Professor Ron Ferguson summed it up best in his work *How High Schools Become Exemplary* when he said, "The main lesson was that student achievement rose when leadership teams focused thoughtfully and relentlessly on improving the quality of instruction." The Literacy Initiative at Brockton High School was well underway, and the results proved that it was a success.

References

Ferguson, Ron (2009). *How high schools become exemplary.* Boston: Achievement Gap Initiative at Harvard University. http://www.agi.harvard.edu/events/2009Conference/2009AGIReport.php

Saphier, Dr. Jon. Research for BetterTeaching in Observing and Analyzing Teaching Techniques: http://www.rbteach.com.

Tovani, Cris (2009). *I read it, but I don't get it.* Portland, ME: Stenhouse Publishers.

Chapter Six

Sustaining Continuous Improvement: Staying the Course

Rigor, Relevance, and Relationships for All Students

That initial year of our Literacy Initiative was challenging, and the challenges came from all sides. Members of the Restructuring Committee learned to develop a thick skin and a ready response to the complaints. We actually discussed how to best reply to some of the most common refrains. The students complained about all of the writing they were doing: "We already did this in my other classes!" they whined. We replied, "Well then, you should be good at it and get an A on this assignment!" That generally produced an eyeroll or teeth-sucking response. The teachers complained about a variety of things. When they said, "It's taking away from teaching my content," we asked them if they needed assistance selecting readings and developing writing assignments that supported their content so that this wouldn't happen. To the comment, "I am not an English teacher," we said, "We're not asking you to be one. We're asking you to teach your subject but use this particular open-response writing format when you do." To the statement, "I don't know why we are bothering to do this; it will never work," we simply said "75% failure means that three quarters of our students will not earn a diploma. We have to try something." It was a long and often difficult year. While we always tried to keep a positive outlook, members of the Restructuring Committee knew that we needed to see some improvement with student MCAS scores. Without improvement, we feared our Literacy Initiative would crumble. The reality was that faculty and student buy-in would only come with results.

Holding Our Breath for the Results

Because Massachusetts contracts with an assessment company to correct the MCAS tests, schools have to wait for the results from the Massachusetts Department of Elementary and Secondary Education. Frankly the wait seemed like an eternity that year. We all returned to school in September, but no results had yet come in. The grumbling quickly began when we shared our literacy goals for the year with the faculty on the first day of school. The buzz of the book-burning incident permeated the faculty rooms. The waiting was excruciating.

Finally the suspense ended the last week in September with a call from Massachusetts Commissioner of Education David Driscoll. Imagine our excitement when he began the call by saying, "Something happened there in Boxer Country. I'm calling to tell you that Brockton High is the most improved school in the Commonwealth of Massachusetts, and I'm coming to announce that to the entire school community!"

The next day the scores were officially sent to the schools and soon after to the media. Only then did the Restructuring Committee breathe a sigh of relief. Our plan had worked even better than we had imagined. In only one year of focusing on the open-response writing initiative, we cut our failure rate nearly in half and dramatically improved the number of students reaching proficiency. In English Language Arts, our failure rate dropped from 41% in 2000 to 23% in 2001. Just as exciting was the increase in the percentage of students reaching proficiency: only 27% were proficient in 2000 and 43% were proficient in 2001. We were even more surprised with the math results. Although we had focused on open-response writing, our math results also demonstrated significant improvement. In math our failure rate dropped from an abysmal 64% to 34%. We also saw a dramatic increase in students reaching proficiency with only 16% proficient in 2000 and 30% proficient in 2001.

Grade 10—English Language Arts

Performance Level	1998	1999	2000	2001
Advanced	2	2	6	14
Proficient	20	22	21	29
Needs Improvement	34	35	32	34
Failing	44	41	41	23

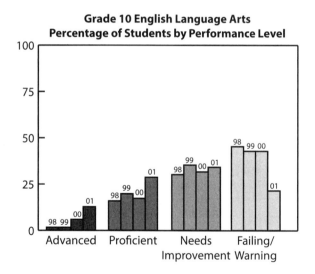

Grade 10 English Language Arts
Percentage of Students by Performance Level

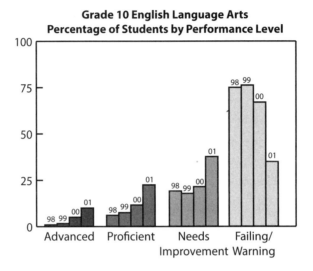

Grade 10 English Language Arts
Percentage of Students by Performance Level

Grade 10—Mathematics

Performance Level	1998	1999	2000	2001
Advanced	1	2	5	8
Proficient	6	7	11	22
Needs Improvement	17	16	21	36
Failing	75	76	64	34

These results were truly beyond our wildest hopes. Just a few months earlier we had been hoping for just a few percentage points of improvement. Now our state commissioner had informed us that we were the most improved school in the Commonwealth of Massachusetts.

We arranged a huge assembly to announce the results. All of our juniors, who had just taken the MCAS in the spring of their sophomore year, were invited along with faculty and administration, elected city officials, and the media. The program opened with our fabulous drum line which got everyone in a celebratory spirit. The superintendent, principal, and associate principal offered a few words of welcome; however, Dr. David Driscoll, Commissioner of Education, became the star of the day when he stepped up to the microphone to announce the state scores and highlight the achievements of Brockton High School.

With enthusiasm and spirit Commissioner Driscoll began his remarks by saying, "Brockton High, you are a School of Champions in your City of Champions!" The students and faculty cheered, and he continued to praise the work of the students who had demonstrated the greatest improvement of any school in the Commonwealth and the faculty who had done such an exceptional job of teaching them. After this moment, we truly had buy-in for our Literacy Initiative.

Building on Success

That moment provided the breakthrough that we needed. Once we had proof that the open-response writing initiative actually worked, we could build on the success. Most of the faculty initially participated in the open-response writing program because they had to, not necessarily because they believed in it. Now that they had seen results, resistance melted. Teachers were on board, and that helped us move forward. Even the defiant ones were essentially silenced by the results.

Now our challenge was to harness the momentum and keep going. We certainly had to continue the writing process but also figure out what we needed to revise and add. While we celebrated our success, the reality was that our failure rate was still a depressing 23% in ELA and 34% in math. Behind every percentage point of failure were the faces of our students who would be denied a diploma. We had a long way to go, but now we had the capital to build on.

Early in the year our Restructuring Committee planned a faculty meeting designed to seek input on next steps in the Literacy Initiative. We divided the faculty into interdisciplinary groups of approximately

15 and provided each teacher with a copy of previously released MCAS tests in both English and math. Our intent was to help all teachers become familiar with the tests and grow their support for literacy.

Members of the Restructuring Committee served as the meeting facilitators. They began by providing approximately 20 minutes for teachers to review both tests and respond to these questions:

- As you look at the MCAS tests in both ELA and math, what do you notice?
- What strikes you about what the students are being asked to do?

After discussing those questions, facilitators asked the teachers what they felt we could do as a school given what they noticed about the test. Finally they asked what each department could do to help the students.

That discussion was among the most productive and positive we had ever conducted with the faculty. The significant improvement in the scores silenced much of the negativity, and the tone of the faculty shifted. Most were now asking what more we could do to help and what our next step was going to be.

After that meeting the Restructuring Committee debriefed and discovered a strong consensus among the faculty about the MCAS tests: students were asked to do a great deal of challenging reading on both the ELA and math tests. The readings were often long, complex, dense nonfiction selections. The faculty requested training to help students learn to access the reading. In the group discussions, teachers of various disciplines admitted that they needed more strategies to help students with reading. As one teacher stated, the only thing she knew to do was tell students to "read it again."

Following the Restructuring Committee debriefing, we sent out a faculty feedback newsletter that shared faculty observations and laid out the plans for the year's Literacy Workshops based upon their suggestions. We would continue the open-response writing initiative according to a calendar of implementation just as we had done the previous year, and we would couple that writing initiative with a series of Literacy Workshops on reading strategies. The faculty was pleased with the direction set by the committee, and the support for the Literacy Initiative grew.

These practices initiated the process that we have now used successfully for a decade. The Restructuring Committee, with faculty input, charts the literacy course for the year. Subcommittees of the Restructuring Committee meet to develop the training scripts and bring the drafts back to the full committee for review. Once the entire Restructuring Committee revises the workshops, the Literacy Workshop is planned for the entire faculty. The targeted literacy skill is modeled for the faculty, and the teachers are well trained to teach the skill to the students.

Year two of our Literacy Initiative continued the focus on the open-response writing and added reading strategies to the teachers' tool boxes. The Restructuring Committee developed a schoolwide Active Reading Strategies format and trained the entire faculty how to use it. (See Chapter 8.) Now when teachers gave their students challenging readings, they first modeled the Active Reading Strategies format and required students to use it. The Active Reading format also became part of the grading process for the writing. Applying these strategies was not optional; it was an important part of improving students' literacy skills and providing them with thinking routines.

The Brockton High faculty became accustomed to these Literacy Workshops. Nearly every faculty meeting was designed as a Literacy Workshop and served as a powerful learning experience for the faculty. No longer were meetings used for administrivia. Over the course of a decade, we developed Literacy Workshops in other Reading, Writing, Speaking, and Reasoning skills. Specific examples of these Literacy Workshops are included in Chapter 8.

This professional development format consisted of the following:

- Restructuring Committee targets the skill.
- Subcommittee of the Restructuring Committee develops the Literacy Workshop.

- Restructuring Committee trains the entire faculty, often by modeling the teaching of the skill in interdisciplinary faculty groups.
- The training is reinforced in a follow-up meeting within departments so that teachers can discuss specific implementation in their own content area.
- Teachers instruct students how to use the literacy skill. For some literacy skills, such as open-response writing, instruction is done according to a calendar of implementation. Others, such as active reading or vocabulary strategies, have no calendar of implementation. These strategies are for students to use and teachers to reinforce on a daily basis.
- Students are required to use the skill and are graded on the process.
- Administration monitors the implementation of these literacy skills through direct observation and collection and review of student work.
- Teachers work together to compare student work.

Each year the Restructuring Committee has targeted one or more literacy skills for instruction. Over the years the workshops have included various literacy skills from all four of our literacy domains: Reading, Writing, Speaking, and Reasoning. Workshops presented include the following:

- Open-Response Writing
- Reading Strategies from Tovani (from *I Read It, but I Don't Get It and Do I Really Have to Teach Reading?*)
- Question Analysis/Active Reading
- Summarizing
- Previewing and Prereading a Text
- Using Visuals to Preview a Text
- Teaching the Text Last
- Thinking About Words: Vocabulary in Context
- Graphing Across the Curriculum

- Multiple Choice Strategies
- Developing Speaking Skills
- Formative and Summative Assessment Strategies
- Problem Solving
- Quick Writes and Foldables
- Developing and Implementing Powerful Openers and Closers
- Reading and Analyzing Visuals
- Vocabulary Strategies (from *Teach Like a Champion*)

The Restructuring Committee has modeled the true meaning of instructional leadership, faculty members have added to their instructional expertise, and students have continued to improve their skills. This approach to teaching literacy has proved again and again to be a success, and the culture of the school has changed. One teacher summarized the shift in culture when she said, "At first we used these literacy strategies because we had to. Now we do it because it works."

Training New Teachers

As this process remains for our faculty, teachers continue to expand their instructional repertoire which benefits our students. However, as in any large organization, faculty turnover is a reality, and we have made sure to get new faculty members trained and up to speed on all of the Literacy Workshops. The Restructuring Committee has determined how best to train our new teachers in a timely fashion and ensure that the training is consistent.

The Instructional Resource Specialists (IRS) conduct the first training on our Literacy Workshops. The district has created the IRS positions to provide support to teachers with instruction in the four testing areas: English, math, science, and social studies. Essentially these are teacher-coach positions. The IRSs teach a reduced schedule and devote the rest of their day to working with teachers, both new and veteran, on instruction. The role of the IRS is to coach, model best practices, provide literacy training, examine student work, and advance the literacy initiative. These IRSs are the first line of training for our new teachers.

Per contract, administration assigns every teacher at Brockton High one duty period per day. That duty period may include assignments such as monitoring the cafeteria, supervising the hallways, or assisting in the offices. With administrative approval, the IRSs pull our new teachers from their administrative duty period on a number of days for literacy training within the first couple of months of the school year. Their participation in literacy training is mandatory and ensures that all teachers new to Brockton High School are trained in all of the literacy initiatives within the first two months of the school year. New teachers then can immediately implement the literacy skills effectively with their students.

As well as the formal literacy trainings scheduled by the IRSs, new teachers are also given support in their classes formally and informally. All first-year teachers are provided a veteran mentor teacher for the year. The mentors work with the new teachers on a variety of issues, not exclusively on the literacy strategies. They counsel, support, and sometimes even comfort the new teacher. New teachers often ask the mentors to assist with planning and even implementing literacy instruction. Because of the extensive network of support, our new faculty members are literacy veterans in no time.

Initiating the Freshmen

Our first-year teachers are not the only newcomers who need to be introduced immediately to our Literacy Initiative. Every year we welcome approximately 1,000 new freshmen to the high school. These young people come to Brockton High from six different middle schools in Brockton as well as from many schools in other communities, even from other countries. We cannot assume that they arrive at the doors of Brockton High with the same middle school experience or academic preparation. Therefore, we introduce these new students to our Literacy Initiative immediately after they become Brockton High students.

The introductory unit begins the second week of school and takes place in the students' history classes. A committee of teachers on the Restructuring Committee and in the Social Science department have worked together to develop these literacy lessons. These lessons demonstrate how instruction in the Literacy Initiative integrates both the literacy skill and the content. History teachers use specific content required by the Massachusetts standards to instruct freshmen on how to use specific literacy skills.

Providing historical context for these literacy lessons reinforces the application of the skills. Teachers begin by introducing freshmen to the mission of literacy using the literacy charts and explaining the school's focus on learning the literacy skills. Then teachers begin the actual instruction using their own content to teach this introductory unit. This unit may last from four days to eight days. Teachers have the flexibility to take the time they need to ensure that all students have mastered the literacy skills being introduced. The unit begins with students learning a pre-reading strategy that they can employ in any class: actively reading a visual. Teachers use any type of visual—graph, chart, political cartoon, or piece of artwork—appropriate for the content of that day. They model the process of actively reading a visual and require students to apply the skill with guided practice and then independently.

The second lesson helps students become more proficient readers by introducing a during-reading strategy: active reading. In this lesson, teachers model the active reading process, and then students follow the five steps to actively read a given text. Because of the importance and complexity of this process, teachers often extend this lesson for an additional day or two.

The third literacy lesson introduces students to effective note-taking strategies to help them become more proficient writers. This post-reading strategy helps students understand the importance of structure and organization in note-taking and focus their idea and notes.

The fourth introductory literacy lesson focuses on assessment, specifically teaching students the skills of summarizing and creating a well-written paragraph. This post-reading strategy teaches students the importance of writing a concise summary, as well as the importance of a well-constructed piece of writing.

These introductory lessons early in the year familiarize freshmen with literacy strategies that they are expected to utilize in all classes. After social science teachers complete these lessons, the department head sends out a message to the entire faculty informing them that the introductory literacy unit has been completed. Students are then expected to use these strategies in every class.

Of course the literacy instruction does not end after the introductory unit. Throughout the year the schoolwide literacy initiatives continue in every class. The process of teaching the skill, implementing the skill in classes according to a schedule, and monitoring implementation through observation and collection and review of student work continues throughout the year.

Brockton High Freshman Literacy Study Skills Unit 2012–2013
This unit introduces freshmen to our Literacy Initiative and teaches them how to implement a number of important literacy skills. Although history classes deliver these lessons, teachers emphasize that the skills being taught are expected in all classes. Each department chair has a copy of the unit so that any teacher of any subject area may review the unit and reinforce these lessons. The entire faculty is notified by email when this literacy unit has been completed so that all teachers can expect the freshmen to apply these literacy skills in all classes.
Lesson 1: READING: Actively Reading a Visual (Day 1) The goal of this lesson is to introduce 9th graders to the strategies used in becoming more proficient readers by employing the pre-reading strategy "Actively Reading a Visual." In this lesson, students will be asked to actively read both a picture and a reading assignment using the four steps in the initiative and answering a question based on their findings. As a schoolwide initiative, students should understand that the strategies used over the course of this lesson should be utilized in all of their classes.

Lesson 2: READING: Active Reading (Day 2)
The goal of this lesson is to introduce 9th graders to the strategies used in becoming more proficient readers by employing the during-reading strategy "Active Reading." In this lesson, students will be asked to follow the five steps to actively read the text they are presented with. As a schoolwide initiative students should understand that the strategies used over the course of this lesson should be utilized in all of their classes.

Lessons 3 and 4: WRITING: Note-Taking/Graphic Organizing (Days 3–4)
Part 1. The goal of this lesson is to introduce 9th graders to effective summarizing strategies as well as introducing them to creating a well-written paragraph. This after-reading strategy will allow students to understand the importance of writing a concise summary, as well as the importance of a well-constructed piece of writing. As a schoolwide initiative, students should understand that the strategies used over the course of this lesson could be utilized in all of their classes.
Part 2. The goal of this lesson is to also introduce 9th graders to effective note-taking strategies and to help them become more proficient writers. This post-reading strategy will allow students to understand the importance of structure and organization in note-taking and help to focus their idea and notes. Though not a schoolwide initiative, students should understand that this strategy can also be utilized in their other classes. (*Note: Teachers may use different graphic organizers or note-taking strategies if desired.*)

Lesson 5: Test-Taking Skills (to be completed by the end of October)
The goal of this lesson is to introduce students to effective test-taking skills that will help them successfully answer multiple-choice and short-response questions. Although a Social Science department initiative, students understand that they may use the strategies in this lesson in all of their classes.

Lesson 6: Map Reading Skills (to be completed by the end of November)
The goal of this lesson is to introduce students to using maps and atlases effectively. This active-reading strategy helps students understand the importance of place and time and adds context in a frame for learning. Although a Social Science department initiative, students understand that they may use the strategies in this lesson in all of their classes.

Lesson 7: Determining Point of View (to be completed by the end of December)
The goal of this lesson is to help students analyze point of view to better understand primary and secondary source documents. This during-reading strategy helps students become more focused readers who understand discourse. Although a Social Science department initiative, students understand that they may use the strategies in this lesson in all of their classes.

Lesson 8: Cause and Effect (to be completed by the end of January)
The goal of this lesson is to help students analyze cause and effect to better understand primary and secondary texts. This during-reading strategy helps students understand what they are reading and determine chronology and causality. Although a Social Science Department initiative, students understand that they may use the strategies in this lesson in all of their classes.

Lesson 9: Understanding Source Documents (to be completed by the end of February)
The goal of this lesson is to help students be evaluative and analytical readers especially when dealing with source documents. This after-reading strategy helps students understand what they are reading and why. Although a Social Science department initiative, students understand that they may use the strategies in this lesson in all of their classes.

Lesson 10: Open-Response Strategies (to be completed by the end of March)
See Brockton High School Initiative.

Lesson 11: Reading Visuals (to be completed by the end of April)
See Brockton High School Initiative.

Critical to the success of the Literacy Initiative at Brockton High School has been the comprehensive and consistent nature of the implementation process. The process ensures that all teachers are appropriately trained and the expectations for instructing all students in these literacy skills are clear. New teachers and new students are trained immediately so that they understand that the culture of the school is using literacy to help students achieve. The Restructuring Committee determines the literacy focus for the year based upon the data and with faculty input. Then a subcommittee of the Restructuring Committee develops the training for the teachers. Teachers are trained in how to teach the students the particular skill and then required to use the skill in their classes. Administration monitors the process carefully using walkthroughs, direct observations, and collection and review of student work. Nothing is left to chance. The results of this approach have led to continued improvement and success for Brockton High students.

Chapter Seven

Advice for the Journey

Rigor, Relevance, and
Relationships for All Students

With each year a new group of 1,000 sophomores faced MCAS testing at Brockton High, so we stayed the course, focused on literacy, maintained the momentum, and continued our improvement. Too often in education changes are simply passing fads. Programs are implemented, and some even produce results; however, a few years later no sign of them can be found. That could not and would not be the case at Brockton High.

Success Breeds More Success

The process we used to implement our Literacy Initiative, as detailed in the previous chapters, has provided the roadmap for our continued success. Our Restructuring Committee examines our student test data to determine our literacy focus for the year. Then a group of committee members determines the steps that a student needs to take to demonstrate that skill. Once they determine the steps involved, committee members develop a training script for a Literacy Workshop to present to the faculty. This Literacy Workshop models for all teachers how to teach the targeted literacy skill to the students. Finally we schedule implementation and monitoring of the targeted skill. This process has been repeated again and again, helping Brockton High continue to improve. Many of the scripts we have developed are included in Chapter Eight. However, even when we introduce new literacy skills, we maintain focus on the ones we have already covered. We continue to help our students build their skills and help our faculty add to their instructional tool box.

After beginning with open-response writing, we added active reading, and again our scores improved. In ELA in 2000 our failure rate was 41%, and our percentage of students reaching proficiency was only 27%. After one year of open-response writing during the 2000–2001 school year, our failure rate dropped to 23%, and our percentage of students reaching proficiency increased to 43%. This was amazing improvement. During the 2001–2002 school year, we repeated the open-response writing implementation and added active reading strategies. We were thrilled to announce our MCAS scores that year. In ELA our failure rate for 2002 dropped dramatically to only 13%, beating the Massachusetts state failure rate of 14%. Also impressive was the increase in the number of students reaching proficiency: 63% of our students scored proficient or above, which beat the state percentage of 59%. We were cheering!

These early years of improvement definitely boosted our faculty's commitment to the Literacy Initiative. Success truly does breed more success. With each year of improvement came a growing sense of belief in the students. Some of the negative and even nasty comments from previous years were silenced and replaced by requests for more strategies. The culture of the school was changing. Each year we added more literacy strategies to support our focus on reading and writing. We always continued the open-response writing supported by active reading strategies. We also provided some vocabulary strategies; the book we had given the faculty, *I Read It, but I Don't Get It* by Cris Tovani, became the basis for many of our vocabulary strategies. Despite the book burning that had occurred at the end of our first year of the Literacy Initiative, we persevered and continued to incorporate Tovani's strategies into our faculty trainings. Each year brought more improvement.

While not increasing at the same rate as the English scores, our math scores also improved. Our failure rate decreased from a dismal 50% in 2000 to 34% in 2001. Our percentage of students reaching proficiency increased from 16% in 2000, with 0% scoring at the advanced level, to 30% in 2001, with 8% reaching the advanced level. We were pleased to see improvement but disappointed that the progress in math was much slower than in English. We knew that we had to develop some math literacy initiatives to help our students. Having witnessed the improvement in ELA, we were eager to try some math initiatives across the curriculum.

The Restructuring Committee spent the 2004–2005 year planning for the schoolwide math initiative Graphing Across the Curriculum. We have included that script in Chapter Eight. We selected graphing as the targeted skill for a couple of reasons. First, it was one of our specific Reasoning Skills, and we had not yet completed a schoolwide Literacy Initiative within the Reasoning Chart. The first skill listed on our Reasoning Chart was "to create, interpret, and explain a table, chart, or graph." Also, the Restructuring Committee had discussed and recognized the need to help the math department get the entire faculty involved in supporting an initiative that would improve students' math skills.

However, we realized that the math initiative would make many faculty members more nervous than the reading and writing initiatives had. We were prepared to hear comments like, "I was never good at math myself. I don't know what they expect me to do." We needed to target a skill that would transfer relatively easily across the curriculum and could be incorporated into any classroom with appropriate training. Most importantly, we realized that when our initiatives were an essential part of every classroom, student performance improved. With every teacher in every classroom targeting and reinforcing the same literacy skill, we gave the students deliberate practice that prepared them well and promoted ownership among the faculty. We wanted to encourage that for math, and we believed that Graphing Across the Curriculum would promote that ownership and improve our students' skills.

When we introduced the Graphing Across the Curriculum literacy training, we followed the same process that we had always employed. Our Restructuring Committee developed a training script detailing the procedures that the faculty would use to teach the students how to analyze and create a table, chart, or graph. Teachers were placed in interdisciplinary groups to learn the important components of tables, charts, and graphs and to analyze and create them with guided practice. We then modeled for the faculty how to teach these skills to the students. Our math department was enthusiastic about this literacy training, and they felt supported by the entire school.

In a follow-up meeting, teachers met in their own content area departments to work out how to select appropriate materials to use for graphing implementation. Members of the math department attended other department meetings to provide support. While overall the faculty had a great spirit about trying this literacy activity, some had apprehension about doing this in every class. Incorporating reading and writing skills into all subject areas seemed much easier than incorporating the graphing. However, teachers now worked together well, and the collegial support was critical to the success of this training. After two literacy workshops on graphing, we were ready to implement the strategy across the curriculum using a calendar of implementation. Every few weeks students had a lesson incorporating a table, chart, or graph. Teachers very creatively incorporated the strategy in every class, and by spring the students had been taught the lesson multiple times. Now we just had to hope that the students transferred the graphing skills they had been taught in their classes to the MCAS testing situation.

Prior to our implementation of the Graphing Across the Curriculum initiative in 2005, our ELA scores were soaring, but our math scores remained low. Our MCAS math failure rate was 29% with only 38% of students reaching proficiency. For the entire 2005–2006 year we implemented the Graphing Across the Curriculum literacy initiative as well as continued with our other strategies in active reading, comprehension, and vocabulary. You could feel across the school an undercurrent of "Please let this work!" as we held our breath while we waited for the results. When scores came in, cheers erupted. Our failure rate in math decreased from 29% to 20%, and our percentage of student reaching proficiency soared from 38% to 52%. We were convinced that the graphing initiative had worked.

We have revisited the graphing workshop a few times, revising it and raising the rigor of what we ask students to do. The graphing workshop also became the basis for one of our most powerful and successful literacy workshops—Reading and Analyzing Visuals (2011), which is included in Chapter Eight. The concept of teaching literacy, including reasoning skills, across the curriculum has always been our core belief.

Note that our Literacy Initiative is not simply to improve test scores. We are committed to providing our students with the skills that they need to be successful in their classes, in college, and in their careers. These are also the skills present in the Common Core State Standards. These literacy skills are not just school skills; they are life skills.

One of our most highly rated literacy workshops had nothing to do with MCAS scores at all. To address our Literacy in Speaking objectives, the Restructuring Committee developed a workshop titled Developing Students' Speaking Skills. We noticed that students were not speaking in class, and when they did, they struggled with how to professionally present themselves. They needed to learn the difference between street talk and school talk. We were also concerned, based upon our many classroom observations, that teacher talk still dominated too many classrooms. The Restructuring Committee wanted to develop a workshop that provided teachers with specific strategies to promote class discussions and provide students with presentation standards.

In this powerful workshop, which is included in Chapter Eight, teachers were trained in three different strategies for organizing class discussions: four corners, inner-outer circle, and graded full-class discussions. The workshop concluded with instruction on an oral presentation rubric that all teachers were asked to try for class presentations. The Restructuring Committee, with input from faculty and students, developed this rubric for schoolwide use; however, prior to requiring this rubric to be used, we wanted teachers to try it and provide the committee feedback. This literacy workshop was an excellent example of providing teachers with instructional tools.

No calendar of implementation was needed. Developing Students' Speaking Skills strengthened teachers' instructional strategies.

As each year began, the Restructuring Committee unveiled new literacy skills to target throughout the year. This approach—targeting a skill based on data, developing a training script on teaching the skill, training all teachers, implementing a schedule, and monitoring the process—has been the roadmap for Brockton High's success. This process has demonstrated that improving student achievement is really more about the faculty, not the students. When we learned to teach the literacy skills, students started doing better.

It's All Good News

The results of our tenacious focus on literacy continue to produce improvement year after year. Brockton High has demonstrated that schools can defy challenging demographics, students can reach high standards, and improvement can be sustained. With this improvement have come many awards and recognitions for our students' academic achievements. Of course we are still very proud of our athletic and performing arts successes, and we all cheer loudly at every tournament game and concert. However, changing our mission and focus of the school to celebrate academic achievement has made external recognition of our hard work and improvement particularly satisfying.

After Massachusetts Commissioner of Education David Driscoll visited Brockton High in the fall of 2001 to announce that we were the most improved school in the Commonwealth of Massachusetts, the accolades continued. In 2002 we were selected by the Massachusetts Department of Education as a Massachusetts Compass School for our improvement. In the literature developed by the Department of Education announcing the selection of the Compass Schools, the DOE wrote, "The Restructuring Committee at Brockton High School attacked the problem of its students' low performance on the MCAS tests with an effective 'home-grown' schoolwide literacy initiative. The initiative targets key skill deficiencies identified through analysis of student performance data and cuts across all content areas...The effectiveness of the schoolwide implementation of the open-ended response writing component of their literacy development model demonstrates the power of a committed staff working together toward a focused academic goal for their students."

Also due to our improved Advanced Placement Scores in calculus, biology, and physics in 2002–2003, we were recognized by the Siemens Foundation for the high participation and passing rate of our students, our open enrollment policy in AP, and our increasing participation of students of color.

In the fall of 2003, the Massachusetts Department of Education informed us that Brockton High had been nominated to be a National Model School. Soon we were contacted by a team from the International Center for Leadership in Education, and that was the beginning of our productive partnership with ICLE. After a site visit from an ICLE educational visiting team, we were selected as one of their model schools; in 2004 we were off to Washington, D.C., to present at the Model Schools Conference.

Our first Model Schools Conference was a powerful professional development experience for the team of teachers and administrators we brought from Brockton High. We were both presenters and learners at the conference. The presentations by Dr. Bill Daggett and his team of experts from ICLE were inspiring, and we immediately embraced ICLE's three Rs: rigor, relevance, and relationships. When our team returned from the 2004 Model Schools Conference, we were filled with ideas and enthusiasm and ready to push forward. For each of the past ten years, we have been proud to have been selected by ICLE as a Model School. Each year that we have presented at the Model Schools Conference, we have come away with many new ideas and strategies to adapt and implement.

We were thrilled in December 2004 to be highlighted by the Commonwealth of Massachusetts again. This time Governor Mitt Romney stood with Commissioner Driscoll at Brockton High to announce and award his newly created John and Abigail Adams Scholarships; this scholarship provided four years full tuition to any Massachusetts state college or university and was earned by outstanding MCAS performance. The Governor chose Brockton High School to announce this new scholarship initiative because we had defied the demographics again and outperformed other schools across Massachusetts. In 2005 at Brockton High 22% of the senior class earned this distinction—comparable to any high school in the state, whether urban, suburban, or affluent. However, while only approximately 5% of students in Massachusetts receiving the Adams Scholarship were students of color, that percentage was nearly 40% at Brockton High. We are proud that our percentage of students earning the Adams Scholarship has increased every year. For the past two years, 33% of our seniors have won this prestigious scholarship, and over half of the recipients have been students of color and poverty.

The awards, recognitions, and positive media stories have kept coming our way. In 2006 we were proud to be one of only six schools in the country to receive the National School Change Award from Fordham University. In January 2008 we were excited to learn that we had been selected as a Bronze Medal winner by *U.S. News and World Report's* America's Best High Schools. We continued to feel honored when *U.S. News and World Report* selected us three more times, in 2010, 2012, and 2013.

Locally, our city newspaper *The Enterprise* offered us a full page every Thursday titled Boxer Roundup. Here we spread positive news about our students' achievements across the city. In 2008 we were also featured by the Boston television show *Chronicle*. This 30-minute nightly news show is highly regarded across New England, and we began to receive wonderful emails and notes from Brockton alumni and former Brocktonians who expressed great pride in the school's turnaround.

In 2009 Harvard Professor Ronald Ferguson released his national Achievement Gap Institute Report titled *How High Schools Become Exemplary*, and we were one of the 15 featured schools. This report really placed us in the national spotlight. Ferguson designed research to find schools that had unusually high value-added test score gains and had narrowed the gaps in test scores between each of their racial/ethnic groups and white students. Ferguson's analysis states, "when Brockton's gains from 8th grade to 10th grade are compared to those of other high schools in the state, the school ranks above the 90th percentile—performing better than 90% of other schools." We presented with Professor Ferguson at his 2009 Achievement Gap Institute at

Harvard in June, and we received tremendous response about how we implemented our Literacy Initiative.

Because of our impressive achievements, Governor Deval Patrick joined new Commissioner of Education Mitchell Chester on the auditorium stage in September 2009 to announce the state's MCAS scores and highlight the success of the students at Brockton High. Our fabulous drum line kicked off the assembly, but our junior class of scholars was the real star of the show. Covering the event was James Vaznis, a reporter from the *Boston Globe*. Vaznis decided to write a follow-up story on the success at Brockton High; ironically it made the front page of the *Globe* almost exactly ten years after we had previously been there as one of Massachusetts's failing schools. Reading the headline "Turnaround at Brockton High" was a great feeling! Governor Patrick invited a group of us to attend his State of the Commonwealth Address, and he concluded his speech by talking about Brockton High. It was a proud moment for us all.

Soon we were featured on a number of Boston area television stations, and then we were contacted by writer Erik Robelen from the journal *Education Week*. For the Quality Counts edition on January 14, 2010, Robelen was writing a piece on standards and assessments. He highlighted Brockton High for its achievement particularly with our many subgroups stating, "In addition, the school met state performance targets last year for all subgroups of students required under the federal No Child Left Behind Act, such as groupings by race and socioeconomic status. The state education agency said that Brockton High's MCAS performance was among the strongest in the state for a school with its low-income demographic."

We continued to have a dynamic and exciting year in 2010. The National Association of Secondary School Principals and the Center for Secondary School Redesign selected us to present at their School Showcase at the NASSP Annual Convention. We received this honor again in 2011. However, the most exciting news was yet to come.

Just after school started in September 2010, we received a call from Sam Dillon, a reporter from the *New York Times* who told us that he wanted to do a story on Brockton High. A decade ago we were on the front page of the *Globe* as one of the lowest performing schools in Massachusetts, and now we were being featured by the *New York Times* for achievement! The article ran on the front page of the *Times* on September 28, 2010, and the positive response was incredible.

Following the article in the *New York Times*, we were featured on a segment on *CBS Evening News* which ran on November 14. The segment focused on the impact of the Literacy Initiative in our success. We were then invited to present in New York City at the Celebration of Teaching and were even highlighted on CNN.

We were very proud when the Associated Industries of Massachusetts (AIM) honored us by presenting Brockton High with the prestigious Gould Award. "Over the past 14 years the Gould Award has gone to individuals, employers, higher education institutions, a foundation and a training provider—this is the first time we have recognized a school," said Richard C. Lord, AIM's President and CEO. "We honor Brockton High School for what it has accomplished through hard work and high expectations—and for its example of what that kind of commitment can achieve in our public schools."

The 2012–2013 academic year began with great news. Our continued improvement, particularly the achievement of our students with disabilities, English language learners, and students receiving free and reduced price lunch, resulted in the Massachusetts Department of Elementary and Secondary Education giving Brockton High a Level 1 ranking, indicating that we were meeting gap-narrowing goals. While not as glamorous as the *CBS Evening News* or the *New York Times*, a Level 1 ranking validated the success of the school and provided us with tremendous credibility.

Brockton High School 2012 Accountability Data		
This school's progress toward narrowing proficiency gaps (Cumulative Progress and Performance Index: 1–100)		
Student Group	Performance Index (On Target = 75 or Higher)	Analysis
All Students	87	Met Target
High Needs	86	Met Target
Low Income	88	Met Target
ELL and Former ELL	80	Met Target
Students With Disabilities	60	Did Not Meet Target
African American/Black	85	Met Target
Hispanic/Latino	88	Met Target
White	89	Met Target
Accountability and Assistance Level: Level 1 Meeting Gap Narrowing Goals		

The pride in the school has continued to grow. With every award and honor we receive, we produce a huge banner announcing the award and display it in the main entrance of the school. As visitors enter our reception area, they find themselves facing banners proclaiming Brockton High as a National Model School, one of America's Best High Schools, recipient of the National School Change Award, recipient of AIM Gould Award for Excellence, and Harvard's Achievement Gap Institute Exemplary High School. Long gone are the days of being on the front page of the *Boston Globe* as one of the worst high schools in Massachusetts.

However, perhaps the greatest recognition comes every year on the first Saturday in June when our football field is the site of our greatest victory—graduation. Every year nearly 900 graduates march proudly into Marciano Stadium at Brockton High School and truly demonstrate that they are champions. The stadium stands are filled with the families and friends of the graduates celebrating this wonderful achievement. While we deeply value all of the external awards and recognitions we have received, we most deeply value the recognition that comes from our graduates and their families for playing a role in their success.

Brockton High School has undertaken a comprehensive redesign process by implementing a schoolwide Literacy Initiative that has resulted in significant improvement in student achievement. All constituent groups have a strong feeling that a positive and significant cultural change has taken place. One of our administrators who had been at Brockton High for over 35 years referred to the change in philosophy as a sense of responsibility for the learning of all students. In a statement he wrote in preparation for a visiting team coming to Brockton High, he clearly articulated the perceptions and beliefs across the school regarding the positive change: "The students, teachers, and administrators have a firm commitment to continue making changes to improve the school. We realize that we are a work in progress. Though uncomfortable at times, we are not afraid to fail. This makes Brockton High an exciting place in which to learn and to teach."

The story of Brockton High—its evolution from a traditional high school celebrating athletics and performing arts to one celebrating the academic achievements of the students—is truly a narrative of continuous change. Perhaps the most significant change has come with a belief in the possibilities, opportunities, and positive spirit that this significant redesign creates in the school. Making change like this takes real tenacity, not brilliance, and what we accomplished at Brockton High is replicable and sustainable. Brockton High School continues to champion a *High Standards, High Expectations, No Excuses* philosophy.

For What It's Worth: Advice for your Journey

Look up educational leadership on Amazon and you will find thousands of books written on the subject. They are written by scholars, professors, and researchers, and their theories are backed by university studies, surveys, and interviews. So what can I possibly add to those thousands of books? This final section offers no surveys, no studies, and no university research. Rather, this is my Top Ten list shaped by my nearly 40 years of service at Brockton High as a history teacher, department head, housemaster, associate principal, and principal. I would call these my "Lessons Learned the Hard Way." These are the bits of wisdom that no graduate course in education and no administrative training program ever taught me. The overarching theme of this entire section reflects my belief that making change takes tenacity. This is my "Walk a Mile in my Shoes" advice. Take it for what it's worth.

1. **Change happens in a school; it cannot be brought about by Central Office**. With all due respect to any central office administrator or school board member reading this, you cannot make us change. The teachers and administrators in the schools are the key to making change happen. From the Central Office you can help us by providing the support and resources we need. You can stand behind us when the complaints come in. You can recognize and honor our success. However, when you present us with five-year plans filled with a million goals and objectives, we will probably not share your enthusiasm about working toward those goals. They are your goals—not ours— and we will likely manage to derail them.

2. **It takes a team to implement change.** The Lone Ranger exists only in movies and on television; no one can bring about the change that many schools need alone. However, people are often reluctant to step forward and join that team. Go after those people, even if you have to beg or drag them on board kicking and screaming. When we began our Restructuring Committee, the culture in the school was so toxic that teachers who joined didn't even want their colleagues to know they were part of the committee. However, their ideas, insight, and commitment to improving the school were the reasons we succeeded. Your best hope for moving your school forward may be to work with the experts within your own school.

3. **Focus, focus, focus. Make literacy your target, and begin with writing.** Prior to the implementation of our Literacy Initiative, the quality of education a student received at

Brockton High depended totally upon the teachers he or she had. We did not have schoolwide standards of excellence; every classroom was like a separate school. As we faced the demands of Massachusetts state standards and the MCAS test, we realized that we needed a schoolwide focus to help our students succeed. When we identified our literacy skills— Reading, Writing, Speaking, and Reasoning—and trained the faculty to teach the students how to use these skills, student performance improved. We began with writing because writing is thinking. That gave us our focus, and our leadership has targeted literacy no matter how many people have tried to pull us away for another program or idea. Yes, we have had new superintendents and directors come in with different initiatives. However, we have stayed the course, tuned out the noise, and gone full steam ahead with literacy. Our improved scores from our Literacy Initiative have given us the clout to maintain our tenacious focus. In addition, the Common Core State Standards are organized around literacy. Focus on literacy, particularly reading and writing, and stay the course.

4. **You want to improve your school? It's about instruction!** The key to our success had nothing to do with the students. It was about adult learning. When we learned to teach the students differently, they started doing better. Educational literature is filled with research to support the power of instruction. We recognized that these literacy skills and thinking routines first needed to be taught to the teachers. Most educators hadn't received this type of training in their teacher preparation programs. For example, during my years of teaching history, I incorporated many primary source documents and challenging readings with which students sometimes struggled. When the students told me they didn't understand, I thought I was teaching reading by saying, "Well then, read it again!" When I learned how to teach the students strategies to actively read, they did better. Our students' improvement corresponded with the faculty's improved instructional skills. The key to our success was adult learning.

5. **Implement with a plan; leave nothing to chance.** Too often teachers go to conferences or attend professional development workshops with little follow-up. If what you are doing is important, then *all* students deserve it. When we began our Literacy Initiative and trained everyone in open-response writing, we knew that some teachers would incorporate it immediately, others would do it once, and many would never do it. The strength in our plan was assigning teachers to particular weeks to implement the writing. That provided students with repeated, deliberate practice over time, and as a result, they learned it. More importantly, no one was exempt. We found success by saying, "We *all* do it this way."

6. **What gets monitored is what gets done!** Just as the implementation needed to be well planned to ensure quality learning experiences for the students, the implementation also needed to be closely monitored to ensure that it was being done consistently and well. We strictly monitored the implementation by observing instruction and collecting and reviewing student work. Administrative presence in the classrooms during our literacy implementations reinforced for the teachers and the students in the school that this was important. Collecting and reviewing student work was the key to raising rigor across the school. Some teachers did not believe that students could do it until after they saw the evidence. Having structured discussions comparing student work helped to raise rigor.

7. **You will *always* face resisters and naysayers. They key is how you deal with them.** Each situation needs to be handled differently, but the key is that it must be handled. You cannot allow people to opt out of schoolwide initiatives. In most cases you can persuade people by clearly explaining why something is being done. However, no explanation or evidence might ever convince the most difficult resister. In these cases, use specific, clear directives. If directives are not followed, take disciplinary action. Disciplinary action is certainly not what anyone wants or enjoys, but it may be necessary.

8. **Celebrate and publicize your successes, even small ones.** We had always celebrated our athletic victories with pep rallies, displayed trophies, and hanging banners. When we had our first year of improvement, we had our first of many academic rallies. All the students were brought to the auditorium, the drum line got the place rocking, and we invited our city officials to share in the celebration. In addition to holding these academic rallies, we also aggressively contact the media: we inform our local newspaper and cable TV station about our celebrations. Using the media in this way is important; you are your best marketing agent. We also celebrate academic achievements throughout the school year. Each term students who make the Honor Roll are treated to a very special and always entertaining assembly by principal's invitation. Whenever we demonstrate improvement in our scores, we celebrate and make sure the students and their parents know. For the Adams Scholarships, we invite all of the scholars, their families, and school and city officials to an assembly in which each student receives his or her scholarship. At the conclusion of the program, we bring all of the Adams Scholars together for a group photograph that we put on a billboard on a local highway. Honoring the faculty is also an important part of our culture. After 20 years of teaching at Brockton High, teachers become a Boxer Faculty Champion; at our convocation they are brought up on stage and presented with a laptop case that is personalized and embroidered with their names and our Brockton Boxer logo. These teachers are greatly applauded by their colleagues. This kind of celebration and notoriety is important.

9. **Leadership matters—a *lot*.** What is leadership anyway? To me *leadership* means getting others to do what they need to do when either they can't or won't. Making a case for the needed change and creating a positive, supportive culture focused on results is essential. For teachers, that means stepping up when something needs to get done. You may not have a strong principal or superintendent, but that can't be an excuse

for inertia. Our Restructuring Committee was an example of teacher leadership. Members set the course, modeled best practices, trained their colleagues, and ensured results. For administrators, remember that with authority comes great responsibility. Charting the course and getting everyone to pull in the same direction may not be easy, but it is essential. Remember the four steps in our turnaround: empower a team, focus on literacy, implement with fidelity, and monitor fiercely. Every step of that path required strong leadership. When the naysayers and resisters surface, accept that challenge and confront the problem. Leadership requires courage and skill.

10. **No excuses: life isn't fair. Use the challenges to your advantage. Changing expectations is *free*!** When *Boston Globe* reporter James Vaznis wrote his article about our school's turnaround, he began the story by saying, "Brockton High School has every excuse for failure, serving a city plagued by crime, poverty, housing foreclosures, and homelessness." While we may have had every excuse for failure, we would not accept failure—not anymore. Initially our students didn't believe in themselves. Many of our students are the first in their families to graduate from high school, and most are first in their families to go to college. The school is an important influence to make students believe. Before we could get the students to believe in themselves, we had to get the adults to believe, and the adults needed proof. They got their proof when we saw the improvement. We used the views of others to light a fire under our students. We shared with them the negative comments and articles so that they would work harder. As students began to succeed, everyone believed; most importantly, the students believed. Their pride came from the solid literacy skills that they had learned to practice and demonstrate. Not only did the students' and the faculty's expectations about achievement change, but the city's expectations of their high school also changed. When I first became the associate principal, a salesperson from a local store asked me if I wore a bulletproof vest to school and told me that she would pray

for me! In one of our city's newsletters, a city resident referred to us as the city's cesspool. Today our city residents and school alumni refer to Brockton High with great pride. Recently a reporter new to the staff of our city newspaper asked me in an interview, "Many local officials, including some on the School Committee, have taken to referring to the high school as 'the jewel of the city.' How do you respond to that?" Of course I agreed wholeheartedly and even suggested to him that we were not just any jewel—we were a diamond. I also smiled to myself at his question. From a cesspool to a jewel: that is a transformation. By embracing a culture of *High Standards, High Expectations, No Excuses*, Brockton High School has truly become a School of Champions.

Chapter Eight

Literacy Workshops

Included in this chapter are samples of the scripts of the Literacy Workshops that we developed to train our faculty in teaching of targeted literacy skills. We have selected sample scripts in all four literacy areas: Reading, Writing, Speaking, and Reasoning. These scripts represent an evolution of our own expertise, and you will notice different formats with these scripts. Over time we became more skilled at developing these workshops. In fact, when we first began these literacy trainings, our technology in the school was extremely limited; we had to use transparencies and overheads. Over time we were able to transition to PowerPoint presentations and videos. The technology we use continues to evolve; however, technology is only the mechanism for delivery of the workshop. As you review these scripts, we hope you see a constant focus on improving instruction for all teachers. When we learned how to teach the literacy skills, our student performance improved.

As you think about using these scripts for your own faculty, consider these recommendations.

1. Bring together a team and read through the script as if you are a participant. Then pull the script apart and make it your own. Of course you can try to use our scripts as is; however, the real power of this process comes when your own teachers develop and deliver these workshops.

2. Remember how we worked. The Restructuring Committee targeted a skill and then developed a training script. We use a PowerPoint presentation for the training, and every presenter uses that presentation. In this section we have tried to provide the narrative of the script, so you are not just seeing a few words on a PowerPoint slide. We hope that you can use the training narrative to follow along with what the presenter is doing. However, make that narrative your own.

3. Because of our teacher contract, our faculty meetings are set by date and time. According to contract, our faculty meetings, which we used for our Literacy Workshops, must be scheduled for the first and third Thursdays of a month. These meetings can only extend for one hour after student dismissal time. Since we had no flexibility on date and time, you will see in our scripts very prescribed times to ensure the workshop ended within the contractual timeframe. If you do not have these types of restrictions, use the time to your advantage.

4. These are working documents, and we have shared them in their original form and in the order that we implemented them. As you review them all, notice how these scripts evolved. For example, the Open-Response Writing Literacy Workshop was the first one we did. It really served two purposes: teaching the faculty the writing process and acquainting them with the rigor and format of the MCAS. The Restructuring Committee members who presented the workshop had never done anything like this before. We were nervous, and all of us wanted a step-by-step script. Now that we have developed our own expertise in presenting these literacy workshops, we do not provide the actual word-for-word directives. Our presenters now use the PowerPoint as their script. We are happy to share these scripts as a guide for you, but please remember that they are works in

progress. Find the balance you need with your own team and faculty.

5. Finally, the specifics of these scripts are not as important as the *process* we used. Simply trying to impose these trainings on your school will result in teachers feeling that another professional development is being done *to* them. I strongly recommend that you follow our process rather than our scripts. Remember the four steps in our transformation: empower a team, focus on literacy for all, implement with fidelity, and monitor fiercely. Remember that no one was exempt from these trainings. If you don't follow the process and engage and empower the faculty, these scripts will be like so many other failed professional development experiences—passing fads that do not take hold. The process is crucial.

Developing a Training Script

To ensure that everyone involved in an initiative is using shared vocabulary and has a common focus, it is useful to develop formal scripts for training.

The Process of Development

Brockton used a careful process to develop scripts that it used to train teachers on new literacy strategies. A restructuring committee of key faculty and staff began by reviewing data and selecting an area of focus.

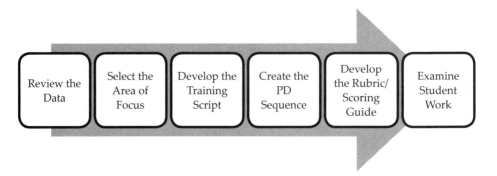

Review the Data → Select the Area of Focus → Develop the Training Script → Create the PD Sequence → Develop the Rubric/Scoring Guide → Examine Student Work

Key Factors in the Training Model

Brockton succeeded with its training scripts because it followed these critical steps.

- A small group of committee members prepared the script to ensure that everyone heard the same message.
- Scripts were tried, then revised based on reactions.
- Instruction on the target issue was expected in all classrooms over time and followed an implementation schedule.
- A common rubric was employed across the disciplines.
- A process of evaluation and feedback was used to determine the level of application in the classroom.
- Positive outcomes were celebrated as student performance increased.

Literacy Skill: Writing
Open-Response Writing

Overview

This training script was the first one our Restructuring Committee developed and implemented. This literacy workshop was designed to instruct the faculty in how to teach the students to respond to an open-response item that may appear on an assessment. It also served to familiarize the faculty with the rigor and content of the actual MCAS test, and develop consistent standards of assessment across the school. Our intent in scripting the training was to ensure that all teachers were trained in the same format so that they could then model the open response writing process for their students. As well as serving to prepare our students for the MCAS, the steps included in the open-response process are aligned with the expectations set by the Common Core State Standards listed below. The steps support students first determining what the question is asking prior to reading the text. This provides a structure for students to write a quality response. It also demonstrates for all teachers how to incorporate the teaching of writing across the curriculum.

Faculty Training Script

Open-Response Writing
Literacy Skill: Writing **Lesson Duration:** 50 minutes **Link to Common Core State Standards** • **CCSS.ELA-Literacy.CCRA.R.1** Read closely to determine what the text says explicitly and to make logical inferences from it; cite specific textual evidence when writing or speaking to support conclusions drawn from the text. • **CCSS.ELA-Literacy.W.9–10.1** Write arguments to support claims in an analysis of substantive topics or texts, using valid reasoning and relevant and sufficient evidence.

Learning Outcomes

As a result of this training, faculty will be able to:

- Implement the writing literacy skill: to write an open response.
- Model the ten steps for open-response writing for their students.
- Instruct their students in the open-response writing process using guided practice and independent practice.
- Apply the ten steps for open-response writing to their content area.
- Assess the students' writing using the Open-Response Writing Rubric.

I. Introduction

Welcome to the open-response writing training. Today we are going to review the ten steps all students must follow when responding to open-response items. We will model the strategy and then you will use it with your students on a regular basis.

Reading key direction words in essay questions is a process that consists of active reading, thinking, and writing. Having your students go through the process rather than just beginning the open response is important. Stress to your students that going through the steps is required, not voluntary; the students should earn credit for the steps as well as credit for the actual open response. At least initially, monitor these steps in class rather than assign them as homework. Even if students indicate that they have done this previously, stress to them that they need to practice this skill. Let's get started.

II. Teaching the Strategy

Ask teachers to review the Key Direction Words. Explain the following:

- *The words listed are used frequently on the MCAS in all four testing areas.*
- *Please use a variety of these words not only on the open-response activity, but also on your tests, homework, and class work.*
- *Whenever possible, please use words from this list with your students.*

Key Direction Words in Essay Questions	
analyze	Break down a problem or situation into separate parts or relationships and examine each part.
apply	Relate a particular idea to a given subject.
compare	Use examples to show how things are similar and different, with greater emphasis on the similarities.
contrast	Use examples to show how things are different in one or more important ways.
define	Clarify meaning by giving a clear, concise definition of a term. Generally, defining consists of identifying the class to which a term belongs and telling how it differs from other things in that class.
describe	Give a detailed sketch or impression of the subject or topic.
discuss	Examine and talk about all sides of a subject or issue in a carefully organized manner.
evaluate	Present your opinion and judgment of something. Explain the criteria you are using to judge something and apply that criteria to specific examples.
explain	Make clear how something (or someone) works, what something (or someone) is like, or why something happens or works the way it does. This term is similar to discuss but places more emphasis on cause-effect relationships or step-by-step sequences.
illustrate	Give examples as a means of explaining your thinking.
predict	Explain what you think will happen, and base that prediction on evidence.
prove	Bring out the truth by providing evidence and facts to back up a point.
state	Present a brief, concise statement of a position, fact, or point of view.
summarize	Present the main points of an issue in a shortened form. Details, illustrations, and examples are usually not given.
trace	Present in step-by-step sequence a series of facts or events that are somehow related. Usually the facts are presented chronologically to show the development of the subject.

Now I will model the ten steps students will use when answering an open-response item.

The following chart includes the training steps that the facilitator will use and an explanation of the work to be done by the participants.

Let's go through the ten steps using The Book of Ruth as our sample text.

Training Steps	Modeling the Strategy
1: Read the question carefully. *Be sure to determine what the question is asking.*	**Question:** After reading the excerpt from Jane Hamilton's novel *The Book of Ruth*, identify the narrator's attitude toward her job at the Trim 'N Tidy Cleaners, and explain how she reveals that attitude. Use relevant and specific evidence from the text to support your response.
2: Circle or understand key words. *In the question, circle or understand key words to stress what the question is asking.*	After reading the excerpt from Jane Hamilton's novel *The Book of Ruth*, (identify) the narrator's attitude toward her job at the Trim 'N Tidy Cleaners, and (explain) how she reveals that attitude. Use (relevant) and specific (evidence from) (the text to support your response.)

3: Restate the question as a thesis. *When restating the question as a thesis, be sure to leave blanks. Essentially the students should flip the question into their thesis statement. This is crucial to the process, and it is an area in which students continue to have difficulty. Complex questions require that students develop more complex thesis statements, perhaps requiring that they write more than one sentence. Please assist students with this process.*	In this excerpt from Jane Hamilton's novel *The Book of Ruth* the narrator shows a _____ attitude toward her job; she is _____, _____, and _____.
4: Read the passage carefully. *Keep the question in mind.*	Refer to the text.
5: Take notes that respond to the question. *Brainstorm and map out your answer. Remind students that they should be doing ACTIVE reading. They should use strategies to develop their answer, such as taking notes, circling and underlining key words, and using brackets. Follow reading strategies developed in the workshops.*	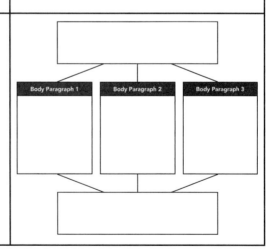

| **6: Complete your thesis.** *This should be based on the student's findings.* | In this excerpt from Jane Hamilton's novel *The Book of Ruth*, the narrator shows a <u>negative</u> attitude toward her job; she is <u>dissatisfied with the work environment</u>, <u>critical of the customers</u>, and <u>unstimulated by her work as a finisher</u>. |

7: Write your response carefully using your map.

In this excerpt from Jane Hamilton's novel *The Book of Ruth*, the narrator shows a negative attitude toward her job; she is **dissatisfied** with the work environment, **critical** of the customers, and **unstimulated** by her work as a finisher.

Body Paragraph 1

Transition: One…

Topic: negative attitude toward her job because she is **dissatisfied** with work environment

Quotation: Par. 2, lines 1–4

Explication:

Wrap-up:

Body Paragraph 2

Transition: The next…

Topic: negative attitude toward her job because she is **critical** of customers

Quotation: Par. 3, lines 9–13

Explication:

Wrap-up:

Body Paragraph 3

Transition: The final…

Topic: negative attitude toward her job because she is **unstimulated** by the work

Quotation: Par. 3, lines 15–17

Explication:

Wrap-up:

To conclude, in this excerpt the narrator, Ruth, expresses a negative attitude toward her job at Trim 'N Tidy Cleaners because she is **dissatisfied** with the work environment, she is **critical** of the customers, and she feels **unstimulated** by her work.

The following open-response structure may be helpful to students as they write their responses.

*Write a **thesis statement** that uses **key words** from the question.*

*Write a **transition** using **key words** from the **thesis statement** to introduce your first **example**, providing some detail or information for the reader about the example. Then, lead into a **quotation** that connects with the example. Follow with an **explanation** that uses **key words** from the **thesis** to **connect** it to the **example** and **quotation**.*

*Write a **transition** using **key words** from the **thesis statement** to introduce your second **example**, providing some detail or information for the reader about the example. Then, lead into a **quotation** that connects with the example. Follow with an **explanation** that uses **key words** from the **thesis** to **connect** it to the **example** and **quotation**.*

*Write a **transition** using **key words** from the **thesis statement** to introduce your third **example**, providing some detail or information for the reader about the example. Then, lead into a **quotation** that connects with the example. Follow with an **explanation** that uses **key words** from the **thesis** to **connect** it to the **example** and **quotation**.*

*Write a concluding statement that repeats the **thesis** and **key words** from the question.*

8: Strategically repeat key words from your thesis in your body and in your end sentence.	In this excerpt from **Jane Hamilton's** novel **The Book of Ruth**, the narrator shows a **negative** attitude toward her job; she is **dissatisfied** with the work environment, **critical** of the customers, and **unstimulated** by her work as a finisher.
9: Paragraph your response. *This is similar to the structure described in step 7.*	**One** example of the narrator's **negative attitude toward her job is her dissatisfaction with the work environment**. She seems to suggest that Trim 'N Tidy Cleaners is a dangerous place to work. She points out that the chemicals used in the cleaning process are **strong enough to wreck buttons**. In addition, she complains about the odor, stating, "…I thought I'd never get used to **the smell**….My breath smelled like dry cleaners….I could feel **the odor** in my mouth…on my teeth…in my chicken soup…behind my eyeballs" (1). Because the narrator gives such specific **complaints** about the environment at the cleaners, she clearly expresses her **negative attitude and her dissatisfaction**.
10: Reread and edit your response. *Students reread their response and make any edits necessary to improve their writing. Be aware of the amount of space students have to answer a question on a standardized test item. Note and inform students that they cannot go beyond the space provided. They can choose to double up lines (two lines of writing within one space), but they cannot go beyond the space provided.*	

The next example of the narrator's **negative attitude** toward her job is her **critical attitude toward the customers** of Trim 'N Tidy Cleaners. She states, "…an **idiotic** girl brought in her bathing suit…" and **continues to criticize** saying, "They **smelled** like cows…they looked **big and dumb**, like being with a **herd**…had made them **mute**" (1). The narrator's comments show that she thinks of the customers as animals. She does not enjoy meeting and talking to them; she does not admire them. Instead, she voices her disrespect and disdain. Clearly, the narrator's **negative attitude toward her job includes her lack of respect for the customers.**

The final example of the narrator's negative attitude toward her job is her boredom and **dissatisfaction** with the work. Her comments make the tasks seem **uninteresting and dull**, and she is not stimulated by the work of a finisher. She states, "…Here goes my life; I'm going to spend the rest of my dying days working at Trim 'N Tidy. I couldn't stand thinking there wasn't anything more left for me…" (1). The narrator's **negative attitude suggests that she believes the job is a waste of her time and a waste of her life.**

To conclude, in this excerpt the narrator, Ruth, expresses a **negative attitude** toward her job at Trim 'N Tidy Cleaners because she is **dissatisfied with the work environment**, she is **critical of the customers**, and she feels **unstimulated by her work**.

III. Review the Steps

After modeling the steps, review them with faculty. Remind teachers to post these steps and have students use them regularly and with consistency.

1. Read question carefully.
2. Circle key words and underline important informations.
3. Restate question as thesis (leaving blanks).
4. Read passage carefully.
5. Take notes that respond to the question. Brainstorm and map out your answer.
6. Complete your thesis.
7. Write your response carefully, using your map as a guide.
8. Strategically repeat key words from thesis in your body and in your end sentence.
9. Paragraph your response.
10. Reread and edit your response.

IV. Assessment

Now we will discuss grading. Typically, state rubrics used to assess open-response items are based on a four-point rubric. For example, a rating of 4 is earned when the response is insightful analysis; a 3 rating is given for general analysis; a 2 rating indicates literal or partial analysis; a 1 rating usually means minimal explanation; and a 0 indicates an incorrect or irrelevant response. Please note that students do not necessarily earn points just for writing something. They can receive a zero for writing a lengthy answer that is off topic. To provide additional guidance for students, Brockton High created a more detailed rubric. We will use this rubric.

Rubric for Open-Response Writing

On pages 110–112 we have provided a BHS rubric that corresponds to the state rubric, one that provides students and you more specific information on criteria that should be included in open-response answers. In regards to this BHS rubric:

- *Answers are evaluated for a clearly stated thesis that answers the question accurately* (point #1 on the BHS rubric).
- *Emphasis is placed on the organization and paragraphing of the response* (point #2 on the BHS rubric). *This helps all students better organize their work and keep their ideas more focused. Students should include two or three specific examples.*
- *The content of the response is important* (point #3 on the BHS rubric). *The examples and information the students provide must be correct. A quality response is well written and correct.*
- *A strong response has specific examples with quotations and clear explanations that connect to the thesis* (point #4 on the BHS rubric).
- *Strategic repetition of key words is emphasized* (point #5 on the BHS rubric). *This technique keeps students focused on the question. For example, if the question asks students to "discuss the attitude of the narrator toward her job" (sample from Book of Ruth excerpt), then students should have the key words negative (or some equivalent) narrator, attitude, and job in their thesis, body paragraphs, and conclusion.*
- *Open responses are not graded on spelling, grammar, and punctuation; however, since clarity of thought is a criterion, clear and complete sentences are emphasized* (point #6 on BHS Rubric). Note: Teachers should not be concerned about spelling errors or minor mechanical errors unless they become so distracting that they interfere with the clarity of thinking.
- *Although no length requirement exists, students should explain their thinking sufficiently and provide appropriate examples with explanation* (point #7 on the BHS Rubric). *Appropriate elaboration impacts the length of their work. In addition, the BHS rubric asks that the work be neat and legible. Again, this is not part of the grading, but we do not want students losing points unnecessarily.*
- *After you have collected the open responses, you may want to do a follow-up lesson and present the class two or three representative student samples showing a high-, middle-, and low-level response (names omitted, of course). Use the BHS rubric to have students score these papers so that everyone sees and agrees upon the criteria. After that, you can use the BHS rubric to score the papers yourself or pair students and have them score each other's papers using the BHS rubric. This may help with grading: students can see what a good paper looks like, and they do much of the correcting.*

> • A high correlation exists between the state rubric and the BHS rubric. At the bottom of the BHS guide, we have assigned point values to the four categories: Advanced, Proficient, Needs Improvement, and Failing. The BHS Advanced correlates to the state 4; BHS Proficient correlates to the 3; BHS Needs Improvement correlates to the 2; BHS failing correlates to the 1. The 0 would be assigned if the student is totally incorrect or off topic.

WRITER'S NAME _____ DATE _____

CONTENT	FORM	
8 • Response contains a clear thesis and insightfully answers all parts of the question. • Response provides relevant and specific textual evidence. • Explanations of evidence are clear and accurate, and demonstrate superior understanding of the material.	**4** • Response contains sophisticated and effective use of transitions and strategic repetition indicating complete control of the material. • Response is logically and effectively organized in its thesis, paragraphing, and sequencing of examples. • Response contains clear sentence structure with few or no errors.	

6	3	LEGIBILITY
• Response contains a clear thesis and adequately answers all parts of the question. • Response provides relevant but general textual evidence. • Explanations of evidence are mostly clear and accurate, and demonstrate good understanding of the material.	• Response contains adequate but simplistic use of transitions and strategic repetition. • Response is organized in its thesis, paragraphing, and sequencing of examples. • Response contains clear sentence structure with no distracting errors.	**1** • Easy to read **0** • Difficult to read
4 • Response contains a thesis but only partially answers the question. • Response provides a mix of accurate and inaccurate textual evidence. • Explanations of evidence are vague and/or demonstrate limited understanding of the material.	**2** • Response contains some inappropriate use of transitions and strategic repetition. • Response demonstrates lapses in the organization of its thesis, paragraphing, and/or sequencing of examples. • Response contains lapses in sentence structure that interfere with the clarity of thought.	

2	1	LENGTH
• Response contains a thesis but only minimally answers the question. • Response provides insufficient and/or largely inaccurate textual evidence. • Explanations of evidence are unclear and/or demonstrate minimal understanding of the material.	• Response contains incorrect or inadequate use of transitions and strategic repetition. • Response reflects minimal organization of its thesis, paragraphing, and/or sequencing of examples. • Response contains major errors in sentence structure.	**1** • Sufficient **0** • Insufficient
0 • Response is incorrect. • Response contains insufficient evidence to show understanding of the material. • Response is off-topic and/or contains irrelevant content.	**0** • Response contains no evidence of transitions and strategic repetition. • Response reflects no organization. • Response contains little to no evidence of sentence structure.	
Evaluated by (circle one): Self Peer Teacher		
Scoring: • 13-14 = Advanced • 11-12 = Proficient • 8-10 = Needs Improvement • 0-7 = Failing	**Total Score**	
Comments:		

V. Summary

Close the training with a summary of the open-response steps and rubric. If appropriate, share the calendar of implementation (see page 41) for when students write open responses in the different disciplines.

Please remember that answering an open response is a PROCESS— consisting of active reading, thinking, and writing. Stress to students that going through the steps is required, not voluntary; they should earn credit for the steps as well as for the actual open response. At least initially, monitor this process in class rather than assign it as homework. Even if students indicate they have done this previously, stress that they need to practice this skill. For many students, particularly when using the process for the first time, instruction may take more than one day.

Literacy Skill: Reading

Active Reading Strategies

Brockton High School leaders developed step-by-step training scripts for those who deliver professional development to staff. The scripts allowed for consistency and coherence in keeping the expectations clearly defined to build staff capacity.

Overview

This training script is a follow-up to the Open-Response Writing workshop. Examining the data revealed that our students had improved their writing skills; however, they needed further support reading the questions, particularly in math. This training session ensures that all teachers model the same active reading process for students. The process consists of students first determining what the question asks them to do and then developing a plan for answering the question. As well as serving to prepare our students for the MCAS, the steps included in the active reading process align with the expectations set by the Common Core State Standards listed below. The process demonstrates for all teachers how to incorporate the teaching of writing across the curriculum.

Faculty Training

Active Reading Strategies: Question Analysis

Literacy Skill: Reading
Lesson Duration: 50 minutes
Link to Common Core State Standards:

- **CCSS.ELA-Literacy.CCRA.R.7** Integrate and evaluate content presented in diverse media and formats, including visually and quantitatively, as well as in words.
- **CCSS.ELA-Reading.I.9–10.2** Determine a central idea of a text and analyze its development over the course of the text, including how it emerges and is shaped and refined by specific details; provide an objective summary of the text.
- **CCSS.ELA-Reading.CCRA.R.4** Interpret words and phrases as they are used in a text, including determining technical, connotative, and figurative meanings, and analyze how specific word choices shape meaning or tone.

Learning Outcomes

As a result of this training, faculty will be able to:

- Implement the reading literacy skills: reading for content; applying pre-reading, during-reading, and post-reading strategies to all reading assignments, including determining purpose and pre-learning vocabulary; understanding a concept and constructing meaning.
- Model for students active reading strategies to help them analyze the question being asked.
- Incorporate active reading strategies into all content areas, for regular use, and especially in test preparation.
- Utilize reading strategies consistently across content areas to assist students in building reading skills and tackling difficult problems.

I. Introduction

We have had success when we address a skill area that needs improvement. Reviewing MCAS results, we see that ELA students attempt to answer the open-response questions because they have been taught across all disciplines in a consistent manner how to approach a response. The result is greater success in that area of the MCAS; however, in math, students still leave many questions blank. This workshop is a response to some of your observations about the math MCAS. The strategy that we will introduce today will help our students break down and analyze questions that they find confusing and overwhelming across the curriculum.

The observations you made in interdisciplinary groups and department meetings about the MCAS math test questions were extremely helpful in focusing the discussion of the Restructuring Committee. We have summarized the observations and would like to take a few minutes to share those findings.

Distribute the Test Observations handout.

Please review the observations focusing on the first two columns of observations.

Share with the group how the *Most Significant Observations* and the *Frequently Mentioned Observations* were compiled at the Restructuring Committee meeting.

At the last Restructuring Committee, facilitators shared their group's findings. We recorded the findings on chart paper and checked those that were repeated. The checks were added up, and the items that received the most checks were placed in the Most Significant Observations column. Those that received more than one check were placed in the Frequently Mentioned Observations column, and those that were mentioned once were placed in the Other Comments Shared column.

Give faculty a few moments to read the observations.

Do you have any other observations that have occurred to you since the last meeting that you would like to share?

Please write down other observations and report them back to the Restructuring Committee.

II. Teaching the Strategy

The next series of faculty meetings will address areas that need our attention to improve students' preparedness on the math MCAS. Note that this is not about trying to get everyone to teach math; this is about improving skills that are transferable to all content areas. One of your observations was that the test demands that students be good readers. Many math teachers who are familiar with the test have observed that even if students know the math being asked, they often cannot break down the questions well enough to know how to answer them.

While there are many active reading strategies, we have selected the following that, when consistently used across all content areas, help build students' reading skills and assist them with tackling difficult math problems. Our goal is for you to try these strategies with your students and provide us with your feedback.

Project the following information.

1. *Read the question.*

2. a. *Circle key direction verbs.*

    For Example—write, draw, explain, compare, show, *and* copy

    b. Underline important information.

    Often some information in a question is irrelevant to finding the answer.

3. *Write what the question is asking you to do in your own words (paraphrase).*

4. *Develop your plan for answering the question.*

III. Modeling the Strategy

Look at math open-response question #21. Model for the group the thought process that a student should go through when following the four-step question analysis.

First, I have to read the question, circling the key direction verbs and underlining important words.

Steps 1 and 2

Read: *Carla can use 100 square feet of floor space in her school's gymnasium, in any way she chooses, to set up computer stations for a science fair. She has chosen to use floor space in the shape of a rectangle, with dimensions that are* **whole numbers.**

I will underline the phrase 100 square feet of floor space. I will also underline shape of a rectangle, dimensions, and whole numbers. Whole numbers must be important because it is in bold letters.

Read: *Part a. Draw all possible rectangles with an area of 100 square feet and whole-number dimensions. Your drawings do not have to be to scale, but you must label the dimensions on each drawing.*

I will circle the word draw and underline possible rectangles, area of 100 square feet, and whole numbers. I will circle the word label and underline dimensions on each drawing.

I notice several important words are repeated: rectangle, area, 100 square feet, and whole numbers.

Read: *Part b. Carla plans to buy a length of rope to surround her floor space. Which rectangle that you drew in Part a. has the smallest perimeter and will thus require the least amount of rope? Show or explain how you got your answer.*

I will underline length of rope and surround floor space. I will underline the words rectangle, Part a., smallest perimeter, and least amount of rope. I will circle show and explain. I will underline how.

Read: *Part c. To set up her computer stations, Carla will subdivide her rectangle floor space into small rectangles that each measure 2 feet by 4 feet.*

I will underline <u>subdivide</u>, <u>rectangle floor space</u>, <u>small rectangles</u>, and <u>2 feet by 4 feet</u>.

> Read: *Using the rectangle you chose in Part b. as Carla's floor space, what is the maximum number of these small rectangles that she can create?*

I will underline <u>Part b</u>, <u>maximum number</u>, and <u>small rectangles</u>. I will circle (is) since in math is often means equals.

> Read: *To support your answer, sketch the rectangle from Part b. subdivided into the maximum number of these small rectangles.*

I will circle the word (sketch) and underline <u>rectangle</u> and <u>Part b</u>. I will circle (subdivide) and underline <u>maximum number</u> and <u>small rectangles</u>.

> Read: *Explain how you know your answer is correct.*

I will circle the word (explain) and underline <u>how</u>, <u>answer</u>, and <u>correct</u>.

Step 3

Now I need to go back and explain **in my own words** what the question is asking. I will try to use different vocabulary, if possible, to demonstrate my understanding.

The first paragraph is setting up the situation; I don't need to do anything there.

For Part a, I need to draw every rectangle with an area of 100 square feet using only whole numbers. Then I have to label the dimensions on each drawing.

For Part b, first, I need to find the distance around (or perimeter of) all the rectangles. Second, I need to choose the rectangle with the shortest distance (or smallest perimeter). Third, I have to show or explain how I got my answer.

For Part c, first, I have to figure out the maximum number of small rectangles that I can make from the big rectangle that I picked from Part b. Second, I have to draw the big rectangle broken up into smaller rectangles. Finally, I have to explain how I know I got the right answer.

Step 4

The next step is for me to plan how I will answer the question. In this case I have created my plan for answering the questions by rewriting them. If I hadn't, I would now develop a plan before answering the questions.

IV. Assessment

Now that I have modeled this process, work with a partner to go through the process using the two math questions provided. Please use the same four steps. You may not be able to come up with the answer, but we want you to feel comfortable with the process. Please model the process with your partner. Please take about five minutes for each person to begin to go through the process. Practice will give you a feel for the procedure.

V. Summary

To conclude, remember the following when using this process with your students:

- Model these strategies for your students using test questions, homework assignments, or a piece of writing in your content area. Remember, you are using readings and assignments in your own subject areas, not create something new.
- Require your students to use these strategies. Provide them with credit for showing the process in their work. Make it a regular expectation for handing in assignments.

We would appreciate your feedback after trying these strategies with your students. Please let us know how they have worked and if you have suggestions for improvement.

Math MCAS Observations

These are comments collected from a previous interdisciplinary small group meeting during which the entire faculty analyzed a math MCAS test.

Most Significant Observation	Frequently Mentioned Observations	Other Comments Shared
1. There is a difficult level of vocabulary on the test. 2. The test demands that students have strong reading skills. 3. There are many problems or questions involving multiple steps. 4. There are many visuals in the test including graphs, charts, and drawings.	1. The test requires strategies for pulling out relevant information. 2. Estimation and approximation show up repeatedly. 3. Students do not know how to use the reference sheet.	1. Students must possess some scientific knowledge. 2. They need to access prior knowledge. 3. They experience difficulty following directions. 4. There is inconsistent math vocabulary used (various terms are used to describe similar or identical concepts). 5. The test requires knowledge of process of elimination and identifying distracters. 6. The majority of the test is algebra and students need to understand the language of algebra. 7. The test requires stamina because of its length and complexity.

Active Reading Strategies Classroom Display

Training participants were given a sheet of active reading strategies to display in their classrooms.

Active Reading Strategies

1. Read the question.

2. a. Circle key direction verbs

   For example: write, draw, explain, compare, show, copy

   b. Underline important information.

   Often some information in a question is irrelevant to finding the answer.

3. In your own words, write what the question is asking you to do.

4. Develop your plan, and answer the question.

Literacy Skill: Reading

Reading for Purpose

Overview

This literacy workshop was designed to review the active reading strategies that teachers were previously trained in and had been using regularly in their classes, and to introduce reading for purpose strategies to better prepare students to attack difficult problems and increase their comprehension. This training script focused on helping teachers improve their students' reading abilities to help the students effectively answer rigorous test questions. The script aligns with the Common Core Standards below. These Reading for Purpose strategies can be utilized across all disciplines to help students break down and analyze questions that they find confusing and overwhelming.

Faculty Training Script

Reading for Purpose
Literacy Skill: Reading **Lesson Duration:** 65 minutes **Link to Common Core State Standards** • **CCSS.ELA-Literacy.CCRA.R.7** Integrate and evaluate content presented in diverse media and formats, including visually and quantitatively, as well as in words • **CCSS.ELA-Reading.I.9-10.2** Determine a central idea of a text and analyze its development over the course of the text, including how it emerges and is shaped and refined by specific details; provide an objective summary of the text. • **CCSS.ELA-Reading.CCRA.R.4** Interpret words and phrases as they are used in a text, including determining technical, connotative, and figurative meanings, and analyze how specific word choices shape meaning or tone.

Learning Outcomes

As a result of this training, faculty will be able to:

- Incorporate active reading strategies into all content areas, for regular use, and especially in test preparation.
- Utilize reading strategies consistently across content areas to assist students in building reading skills and tackling difficult problems
- Describe what active reading is, and the difference between the two most prominent types of active reading used in the classroom.

I. Introduction (5 minutes)

Today's session will address what were identified as some of the areas that we as a school could focus our attention on in an effort to improve students preparedness, especially in terms of test taking. It is important to note that while we will use math examples, this is not about trying to get everyone to teach math but this is about improving skills that are transferable to all content areas. We are using math examples today, as that is an area where students often get lost in reading the question. Using the strategy that we will introduce today across all disciplines will help our students with a way to break down and analyze questions that they find confusing and overwhelming. Our goal is for you to try these strategies with your students and provide us with your feedback.

Begin by asking the following question and having everyone write their answers on note paper: *When you ask students to actively read, what do they do?*

Ask a few volunteers to share out their responses and any reactions to that question.

We're going to talk about a strategy called active reading. When you described what happens when you ask students to "actively read" many students probably look at you with a blank stare and then read a text as they normally would. Let's look at the definition of active reading, and some examples.

II. Teaching the Strategy (10 minutes)

To actively read a text, we can look at three different segments: Question Analysis Reading Strategies, Actively Reading Text, and Summarizing. One way to describe active reading is that students are:
- *Determining the PURPOSE*
- *Doing PURPOSEful reading*
- *Demonstrating comprehension*

Note: Active Reading is much more than circling and underlining.

Let's review what I mean by each of those, first determining the purpose: Active reading of questions, prompts, and directions is a skill used by good readers to determine the PURPOSE of the reading assignment or task.

To determine the purpose of reading, you could use the question analysis reading strategy.

Paraphrase the below, and demonstrate with a real question what you are doing as you read through each step.

These are the question analysis active reading steps:

1. *Read the question.*

2. a. *Circle key direction verbs.*

    For Example—write, draw, explain, compare, show, and copy

   b. Underline important information.

    Often there is information in a question that is irrelevant to finding the answer.

3. *Write what the question is asking you to do in your own words (paraphrase).*
4. *Develop your plan for answering the question.*

III. Modeling the Strategy (20 minutes)

Model for the group the thought processes that a student should go through when following the four question analysis active reading steps.

First, I have to read the question, circling the (key direction verbs) and underlining important words.

Steps 1 and 2:

> Read: *Carla can use 100 square feet of floor space in her school's gymnasium, in any way she chooses, to set up computer stations for a science fair. She has chosen to use floor space in the shape of a rectangle, with dimensions that are* **whole numbers**.

I will underline the phrase 100 square feet of floor space. I will also underline shape of a rectangle, dimensions, and whole numbers. Whole numbers must be important because it is in bold letters.

> Read: *A. Draw all possible rectangles with an area of 100 square feet and whole-number dimensions. Your drawings do not have to be to scale, but you must label the dimensions on each drawing.*

I will circle the word (draw) and underline possible rectangles, area of 100 square feet, whole numbers. I will circle the word (label) and underline dimensions on each drawing.

I notice that there are several important words that are repeated, rectangle, area, 100 square feet, and whole numbers.

> Read: *B. Carla plans to buy a length of rope to surround her floor space. Which rectangle that you drew in part A has the smallest perimeter and will thus require the least amount of rope? Show or explain how you got your answer.*

I will underline length of rope, and surround floor space. I will underline the word rectangle, part a., smallest perimeter, and least amount of rope. I will circle (show) and (explain) I will underline how.

Read: *C. To set up her computer stations, Carla will subdivide her rectangle floor space into small rectangles that each measure 2 feet by 4 feet.*

I will underline <u>subdivide</u>, <u>rectangle floor space</u>, <u>small rectangles</u>, and <u>2 feet by 4 feet</u>.

Read: *Using the rectangle you chose in part B as Carla's floor space, what is the maximum number of these small rectangles that she can create?*

I will underline <u>part b</u>, <u>maximum number</u>, and <u>small rectangles</u>. I will circle (is) (in math, "is" often means "equals").

Read: *To support your answer, sketch the rectangle from part B subdivided into the maximum number of these small rectangles.*

I will circle the word (sketch) and underline <u>rectangle</u> and <u>part B</u>. I will circle (subdivide) and underline <u>maximum number</u> and <u>small rectangles</u>.

Read: *Explain how you know your answer is correct.*

I will circle the word (explain) and underline <u>how</u>, <u>answer</u>, and <u>correct</u>.

Step 3:

Now I need to go back and explain IN MY OWN WORDS what the question is asking. (Encourage students to use different vocabulary, if possible, to demonstrate understanding).

The first paragraph is setting up the situation; I don't need to do anything there.

For Part A, I need to draw every rectangle with an area of 100 square feet using only whole numbers. Then I have to label the dimensions on each drawing.

For Part B, first, I need to find the distance around (or perimeter) all the rectangles. Second, I need to choose the rectangle with the shortest distance (or smallest perimeter). Third, I have to show or explain how I got my answer.

For Part C, first, I have to figure out the maximum number of small rectangles that I can make from the big rectangle that I picked from Part B. Second, I have to draw the big rectangle broken up into smaller rectangles. Finally, I have to explain how I know I got the right answer.

Step 4

Say: *The next step is for me to plan how I will answer the question. I realize that in this case by rewriting the questions I have created my plan for answering them. If not, I would have developed a plan before answering the questions.*

Write your answer to question 21 in the space provided in your Student Answer Booklet.

21. Carla can use 100 spare feet of floor space in her school's gymnasium, in any way she chooses, to set up computer stations for a science fair. She has chosen to use floor space in the shape of a rectangle, with dimensions that are whole numbers.

   A. Draw all possible rectangles with an area of 100 square feet and whole-number dimensions. Your drawings do not have to be to scale, but you must label the dimensions on each drawing.
   B. Carla plans to buy a length of rope to surround her floor space. Which rectangle that you drew in part a. has the smallest perimeter and will thus require the least amount of rope? Show or explain how you got your answer.
   C. To set up her computer stations, Carla will subdivide her rectangular floor space into small rectangles that each measure 2 feet by 4 feet.
      • Using the rectangle you chose in part B as Carla's floor space, what is the maximum number of these small rectangles that she can create?
      • To support your answer, sketch the rectangle from part B subdivided into the maximum number of these small rectangles.
      • Explain how you know your answer is correct.

IV. Review the Strategy (15 minutes)

Say: *Now we would like you work with a partner and go through the process using one of the two math questions provided. Please use the same four steps. You may not be able to come up with the answer, but it is important to feel comfortable with the process. Please model the process with your partner. Please take about five minutes for each person to begin to go through the process. Practice will give you a feel for the procedure.*

Question 17 is an open-response question.
- **BE SURE TO ANSWER AND LABEL ALL PARTS OF THE QUESTION.**
- **Show all your work (diagrams, tables, or computations) in your Student Answer Booklet.**
- **If you do the work in your head, explain in writing how you did the work.**

Write your answer to question 17 in the space provided in your Student Answer Booklet.

17. Quinn works in Chicago and in New York City. He travels by taxi in each of the two cities.

> In Chicago, he pays a fixed taxi fare of $1.90 per ride, plus $1.60 per mile traveled.

   a. Write an equation that expresses f, Quinn's total fare for a taxi ride in Chicago, as a function of m, the number of miles traveled.

> In New York City, Quinn pays a fixed taxi fare of $1.50 per ride, plus 25¢ per 1/10 mile traveled.

   b. Write an equation that expresses f, Quinn's total fare for a taxi ride in New York City, as a function of m, the number of miles traveled.

   c. On a recent trip Quinn noticed that the total number of miles traveled by taxi from the airport to the hotel was the same in each of the two cities. Before tips were added, his taxi fare to the hotel in New York City was $12.20 more than his fare to the hotel in Chicago. What was the distance from the airport to the hotel in each city? Show or explain how you got your answer.

Question 31 is an open-response question.
- **BE SURE TO ANSWER AND LABEL ALL PARTS OF THE QUESTION.**
- Show all your work (diagrams, tables, or computations) in your Student Answer Booklet.
- If you do the work in your head, explain in writing how you did the work.

Write your answer to question 31 in the space provided in your Student Answer Booklet.

A designer at Royal Jewelers wants to create a 10-ounce necklace that will be made of gold and silver. The necklace will have a total value of $206.50.

    a. Write an equation that represents the total weight of the 10-ounce necklace if it contains g ounces of gold and s ounces of silver.

    b. Given that the value of gold is $318 per ounce and the value of silver is $5 per ounce, write an equation in terms of g and s that represents the total value of the 10-ounce necklace.

    c. The two equations from parts a. and b. form a system. Solve the system of equations for g and s. Show all of your work.

    d. What will be the value, in dollars, of the gold in the 10-ounce necklace? Show or explain how you got your answer.

Say: *Now that you've had some practice with active reading, how can determining the purpose improve comprehension?*

Ask for a few volunteers to share what they found during the practice and what role it had on their comprehension.

Let's look at the two other pieces of active reading, doing purposeful reading and demonstrating comprehension.

What do I mean by "doing purposeful reading"?

Paraphrase these points:
- Active reading targets the determined purpose.
- It is the implementation of strategies used by good readers to improve comprehension.
- Active reading is "Proof of DOING"!

Let's review a list of what "good readers do" according to Tovani:
- *Good readers read for different purposes.*
- *Good readers know their purpose.*
- *Good readers ask questions when they read in order to help themselves make inferences.*
- *Good readers connect new knowledge to known information.*
- *Good readers recognize confusion and know how to repair meaning.*
- *Good readers look for organizational patterns in the text.*
- *Good readers make and check predictions.*
- *Good readers not only mark up the text, but describe their thinking.*
- *Good readers are aware of their thinking.*
- *Good readers use tools to "hold on" to their thinking so they can return to it later.*

IV. Assessment (10 minutes)

Say: *To wrap up this session on active reading strategies we'll look at the final component, demonstrating comprehension. There are many ways students can demonstrate comprehension, but one way is through summarizing. Let's have a group brainstorm and summary on how have we asked you, as "students" in this workshop, to demonstrate comprehension of the prompt and the article.*

I'd like you to work with a new partner who did the opposite question than you, and have your partner review your work and offer any additional suggestions, feedback, or items that you may have missed. I'll let you know when 5 minutes are up so that you can switch questions.

V. Summary (5 minutes)

As a final activity before you leave, I'd like you to respond in your notes to the following:

- *3 ways the information from this workshop can help my students improve reading comprehension.*
- *2 ways the information from this workshop can help me improve my instruction.*
- *1 difference between Question Analysis Active Reading and Active Reading of Text.*

When you've finished these notes, please share them with a partner.

We'd like to make some suggestions as to how this process may be used with your students:

- *Try out these strategies by modeling them for your students using test questions, homework assignments, or a piece of writing in your content area.*
- *Remember we are asking you to use readings and assignments in your own subject areas, not create something new.*
- *Require your students to use these strategies.*
- *Provide them with credit for showing the process in their work.*
- *Make it a regular expectation for handing in assignments.*

> We are what we have read and how we read it, and no other single activity has the capacity to yield so much education value.
>
> —Lemov

Literacy Skill: Reading
Vocabulary in Context

Overview
This training script focuses on vocabulary strategies to help students learn and apply content-related vocabulary to improve reading comprehension. Teachers learn the steps of the vocabulary activity Thinking About Words to implement it in their classrooms for word retention. These vocabulary strategies are intended to be tools for the teacher to use when introducing and pre-teaching vocabulary. This was not a literacy initiative that required a calendar of implementation. Rather, these are day-to-day strategies designed to help students learn vocabulary and can be applied in any content area. The steps in this activity align with the expectations set by the Common Core State Standards listed below. Teaching content-related vocabulary enhances student understanding across disciplines and helps with test preparation.

Faculty Training Script

Vocabulary in Context

Literacy Skill: Reading
Lesson Duration: 50 minutes
Link to Common Core State Standards
- **CCSS.ELA-Literacy.L.9–10.4** Integrate and evaluate content presented in diverse media and formats, including visually and quantitatively, as well as in words
- **CCSS.ELA-Literacy.L.9–10.4a** Use context (e.g., the overall meaning of a sentence, paragraph, or text; a word's position or function in a sentence) as a clue to the meaning of a word or phrase.
- **CCSS.ELA-Literacy.L.9–10.4b** Identify and correctly use patterns of word changes that indicate different meanings or parts of speech (e.g., analyze, analysis, analytical; advocate, advocacy).
- **CCSS.ELA-Literacy.L.9–10.5** Demonstrate understanding of figurative language, word relationships, and nuances in word meanings.
- **CCSS.ELA-Literacy.L.9–10.5b** Analyze nuances in the meaning of words with similar denotations.

- **CCSS.ELA-Literacy.L.9–10.6** Acquire and use accurately general academic and domain-specific words and phrases, sufficient for reading, writing, speaking, and listening at the college and career readiness level; demonstrate independence in gathering vocabulary knowledge when considering a word or phrase important to comprehension or expression.

Learning Outcomes

As a result of this training, faculty will be able to:

- Implement the reading literacy skills: reading for content; applying pre-reading, during-reading, and post-reading strategies to all reading assignments, including determining purpose and pre-learning vocabulary; understanding a concept and constructing meaning.
- Model for students vocabulary strategies.
- Incorporate vocabulary strategies into all content areas, for regular use, and especially in test preparation.
- Utilize vocabulary strategies consistently across content areas to assist students in building vocabulary and improving comprehension

I. Introduction (2 minutes)

At previous faculty meetings, we have discussed targeting vocabulary as a schoolwide initiative. Two of the most important tests our students face while in high school are the MCAS and the SAT, and vocabulary is a major component of both these exams. Our data show that our students struggle with vocabulary and could benefit from vocabulary development. Broadening our students' vocabulary may help them succeed on these tests as well as support our Literacy Initiative. Therefore, today we're going to discuss the vocabulary activity Thinking about Words, an exercise you can apply in your classrooms using content-related vocabulary. This activity helps students learn and work with new vocabulary as research indicates that the more students actively use these words, the higher their retention rate is. In terms of our Literacy Objectives, this activity targets several areas: for Writing and Speaking, students explain their thinking in complete sentences, and for Reasoning, students identify and explain a pattern. It is important to remember that these are intended to be tools for your instructional toolbox. They may seem time consuming; however, please remember that if you pre-teach vocabulary words that are critical to your students understanding the content you are presenting, their comprehension will increase. You should carefully target those important vocabulary words to apply to these strategies.

II. Teaching the Strategy (10 minutes)

Today we are going to work with a list of words derived from many departments in the school. Please remember that earlier this year we had a faculty meeting in your content areas and asked every department to develop a list of words that you find are critical to your discipline but that your students struggle with. We will continue to use your suggestions as we work on increasing students' vocabulary. For today, we have pulled a sampling of those words and tried to include word choices from every department on a handout we have provided. When you do this activity in your own classroom, the list of words you use will be one that you have generated from a unit you are doing or from a reading that your students are doing. We recommend that students work with a list of important words that you have selected whose correct definitions are provided by either the textbook's glossary or you.

Before looking at the list, let's review the different strategies we will be practicing today: Categories, Opposites, and Sentences.

Briefly review on the slide the three strategies that make up the Thinking About Words activity. We have provided you with a handout of those three strategies for easy reference when you introduce these strategies to your students.

Handout #1: Thinking About Words

DIRECTIONS: You will use the list of vocabulary words you are currently working with to do the following activities.

A. **Categorization:** group words according to similarities.

Directions: Create three categories of at least three words each. Each group must be labeled with a detailed phrase that clearly indicates the nature of the similarity. Be creative!

Example: Words that indicate a person's state of mind when taking MCAS

Nervous
Confident
Depressed

B. Opposites: pair words that are somehow opposite in meaning.

Directions: Create three pairs of words (three sets of two words each) whose meanings are opposite. Write out one complete sentence that clearly explains the nature of the two words' difference. Within that sentence, you must underline the two words, or phrases, that show how the given words are opposite in meaning.

Example: confident–depressed

The first word describes someone who feels good about himself, but the second word describes someone who feels bad about himself.

Please note in the example that the explanatory sentence does NOT simply provide the definition of each word, but instead uses words opposite in meaning (feels good/feels bad) to point out the nature of the difference. Here is another creative example:

Example: thicket–crematorium

The first word describes something that is living, but the second word describes something that is dead.

C. Sentences: Demonstrate your understanding of the meaning and usage of words.

Directions: Write four grammatically correct sentences that each uses a minimum of two words from your list. Your sentence must contain enough detail to show your understanding of each word's meaning and usage. Note: You may change the form and tense of the word if necessary.

Example: Right before the exam started, the straight-A student strolled into the classroom, looking very confident and relaxed.

Example: The doctor warned me that if the pills he prescribed had the negative side effects of making me feel nervous and depressed, that I should immediately stop taking them and call his office.

III. Modeling the Strategy

CATEGORIZATION (12 minutes)

The first activity is called Categorization: Ask your students to give you the definition of the word categorization, which is to group according to similarity. Then model this activity with a simple example: If I gave you the words sunshine, rake, bird, and flower, what category label would you come up with? How could we label these words and indicate the nature of the category? Participants will probably respond, "Words that are associated with a garden" or "Words that may identify aspects of spring or summer."

Now look at the directions and example on the handout: "Create three categories of at least three words each. Each group must be labeled with a detailed phrase that clearly indicates the nature of the similarity. Be creative!" The example category's label is "Words that indicate a person's state of mind when taking MCAS." Notice that although the words nervous, confident, and depressed do not mean the same thing, they all can fit under this label. Remind students to give their labels some detail and to try to be creative. Does anyone have any questions or comments about categorization? **Answer any questions before having participants practice the strategy.**

Directions: Create three categories of at least three words each. Each group must be labeled with a detailed phrase that clearly indicates the nature of the similarity. Be creative!

> *Example: Words that indicate a person's state of mind when taking MCAS*
>
> *Nervous*
> *Confident*
> *Depressed*

Next, pair with a teacher from another discipline. Use the vocabulary words from the "Sample Vocabulary from Previous Faculty Meeting" worksheet to create three categories of at least three words each. Be creative and detailed with your category labels. Here are some additional guidelines for this activity:

- *Each person is responsible for a completed handout.*
- *Each person must participate in the process. I will circulate to check your progress.*

What are we talking about? On the Thursday before school ends?

- *Do not use simplistic categories, such as "Words beginning with the letter p" or "Words with 2 syllables." Also, do not use definitions as category labels.*
- *When you write your category labels, refer to "words," not "things."(i.e., "words that describe a superhero," not "things that describe a superhero.")*
- *When creating your category, focus on the meaning of the words, and don't get hung up on the words being different parts of speech.*
- *After you finish your first category, raise your hand so that I can check your work.*

After five minutes, we will share your pairings.

As pairs come up with categories, ask each member of the pair to explain his or her thinking on at least one word. If the thinking is not clear, ask the pair to re-think the category label or come up with a different word or words to put in the category. Once participants have created at least one category, convene and share examples verbally.

We have heard some creative categories today. When implementing this strategy into your classroom, have your paired students share their categories with the class by writing one category on the board and explaining it to the class. This adds a speaking component to this activity. Next, let's look more closely at the Opposites Strategy.

OPPOSITES (12 minutes)

Opposites is described as pairing words that are somehow opposite in meaning. The directions read as follows: "Create three pairs of words (three sets of two words each) whose meanings are opposite. Write out one complete sentence that clearly explains the nature of the two words' difference. Within that sentence, you must <u>underline</u> the two words, or phrases, that show how the given words are opposite in meaning." The first example pairs the word confident with the word depressed. The explanatory sentence says, "The first word describes someone who <u>feels good</u> about himself, but the second word describes someone who <u>feels bad</u> about himself. Please note in the example that the explanatory sentence does NOT simply provide the definition of each word, but instead uses words opposite in meaning (feels good/feels bad) to point out the nature of the difference." The second example shows how to creatively see opposites: The words thicket and crematorium are paired and explained as follows: "The first word describes something that is <u>living</u>, but the second word describes something that is <u>dead</u>."

Directions: Create three pairs of words (three sets of two words each) whose meanings are opposite. Write out one complete sentence that clearly explains the nature of the two words' difference. Within that sentence, you must <u>underline</u> the two words, or phrases, that show how the given words are opposite in meaning.

   Example: confident–depressed

The first word describes someone who <u>feels good</u> about himself, but the second word describes someone who <u>feels bad</u> about himself.

Please note in the example that the explanatory sentence does NOT simply provide the definition of each word, but instead uses words opposite in meaning (feels good/feels bad) to point out the nature of the difference. Here is another creative example:

   Example: thicket–crematorium

The first word describes something that is <u>living</u>, but the second word describes something that is <u>dead</u>.

You can see that students are NOT asked to write the definition of each word; rather, the students are asked to explain HOW the words are opposite in their meanings. Does anyone have any questions about this second strategy? Pause to allow participants a chance to respond. Answer any questions.

Now work with you partner to come up with three pairs of opposites using the words on the handout. Raise your hand after you have completed the first pair, so that I can check your work. For our purposes today, you'll have about five minutes to do this activity before we share our findings.

Pairing 1. _____   _____
Explanation

Pairing 2. _____   _____
Explanation

Pairing 3. _____   _____
Explanation

As teachers come up with pairs of opposites, ask each member of the pair to explain his or her thinking on how and why, given each word's definition, they are opposite. Also, make sure participants write in complete sentences and underline the opposites. If the thinking is not clear, ask the pair to re-think the explanatory sentence or come up with a different pairing of words. Once participants have finished creating at least one pair of words, convene the group and share examples.

Thanks for sharing your examples. In order to make this a speaking activity in your own class, you can appoint particular pairs to write a designated set of opposites on the board to share and explain with others.

SENTENCES (12 minutes)

This last activity for Thinking About Words asks students to demonstrate their understanding of the meaning and usage of words. Students write four grammatically correct sentences that each uses a minimum of two words from the vocabulary list. As the directions state, sentences must contain enough detail to show understanding of each word's meaning and usage. In other words, students should include enough context clues to demonstrate their understanding of each word. When creating sentences, students may change the form and tense of the words. Also, remind students to underline the two vocabulary words.

Let's take a closer look at the examples. The first example reads, "Right before the exam started, the straight-A student <u>strolled</u> into the classroom, looking very <u>confident</u> and relaxed." Notice that the word relaxed demonstrates the writer's understanding of the vocabulary words. The second example reads, "The doctor warned me that if the pills he prescribed had the negative side effects of making me feel <u>nervous</u> or <u>depressed</u>, that I should immediately stop taking them and call his office." In this sentence, the word negative provides a clue about the meaning of the words.

Directions: Write four grammatically correct sentences that each uses a minimum of two words from your list. Your sentence must contain enough detail to show your understanding of each word's meaning and usage. Note: You may change the form and tense of the word if necessary.

Example: Right before the exam started, the straight-A student <u>strolled</u> into the classroom, looking very <u>confident</u> and relaxed.

Example: The doctor warned me that if the pills he prescribed had the negative side effects of making me feel <u>nervous</u> and <u>depressed</u>, that I should immediately stop taking them and call his office.

Now with your partner come up with four context-rich sentences that each contains two vocabulary words in them. Write the sentences in the remaining spaces on your sheet. I'll circulate to check your sentences and to observe you and your partner creating and writing these sentences. For our purposes today, you'll have about five minutes for this activity before we convene to share findings.

Sentence 1: _____

Sentence 2: _____

Sentence 3: _____

Sentence 4: _____

Once pairs have at least one sentence, convene the group and ask pairs to share their sentences.

Thanks for your hard work. In the classroom, ask students to write one of their sentences on the board and explain how the sentence conveys the meaning of each word. You can also ask other students to identify the details in the sentence that give clues to the words' meanings.

IV. Assessment (4 minutes)

When implementing the Thinking About Words activity, remember these guidelines for assessing student work.

1. *As you circulate, make sure that each member of the pair verbalizes his or her thinking to ensure that not just one student is doing the work.*
2. *Make sure that students keep a copy of the written work, so that if a partner is absent the next day, the other has a copy. Absent students are on their own to complete the section missed on the day they were absent. Students are not allowed to simply copy a partner's work.*

3. *Cut down on the work you have to do by requiring that pairs hand in only one copy with both names on it. Also, as you circulate, put a checkmark next to the items that you have already checked.*
4. *The written portion of this work can be considered for a quiz grade.*
5. *Students can earn additional credit (for example, participation points) for orally presenting one of their examples to the class.*
6. *Make this activity more challenging by not allowing students to use any word on the list more than one time. This would require students to use 23 different words in total.*
7. *If you want, have students only do one portion of this sheet (such as categorization) per day, thereby limiting the amount of time devoted to this activity during a 66-minute period.*

Do you have any questions about the Thinking About Words activity?
Allow participants time to respond.

V. Summary/Ticket to Leave (3 minutes)

The "Thinking About Words" activity helps students learn and apply content-related vocabulary. Vocabulary development is essential for students to improve their reading comprehension skills and build confidence. I am going to hand out to each of you your ticket to leave today's session. **Distribute a notecard to each participant.**

This exit ticket requires you to write two simple things on your notecard:

1. *Please write down the name of your department (NOT your name).*
2. *Then, below that, please write down one remaining question you have about any aspect of today's presentation. I'll collect your tickets as you leave.*

Thank you.

Stand at the door and collect tickets.

Handout #2: Sample Vocabulary From Previous Faculty Meeting

assymetric: a balance in art composition based on an informal relationship

asset: 1. a useful or valuable quality, person, or thing; an advantage or resource: *proved herself an asset to the company*; 2. a valuable item that is owned

vindictive: vengeful; feeling the need to hurt or get back at another

cross-contamination: letting microorganisms from one food get into another

infinitive: the form of a verb without reference to person, number, or tense, usually easily identified by the word to in front of it (e.g., *to go*)

accreditation: doing something at a high enough level that permission is given to continue

physical health: the care of one's body and its ability to meet the demands of daily living

citation: a reference to footnote to a book, magazine, journal article, or another source; contains information necessary to identify and locate the work

battalion: a military unit made up of two or more companies or batteries and a headquarters

abscissa: the x-coordinate of a point on a graph; e.g., point (1, 3) has an abscissa of "1"

binary: characterized by or consisting of two parts or components; twofold; pertains to having two sections or subjects; from Latin *bini*, two by two

aerate: a term used in cookery as a synonym for *sift*

agility: the ability to change body position quickly and under control

affinity: an attractive force between substances or particles

chronology: a sequence of events over time

secede: to leave a group or organization

mollusks: any of a large group of soft-bodied, usually shell-bearing invertebrates, including snails, oysters, clams, etc.

omniscient: having total knowledge; knowing everything

linear: of or resembling a line or lines

utensils: instruments or containers, especially ones used domestically

convection: movement of heat through a liquid or gas

anarchist: a person or group against all form of government

metaphor: a figure of speech in which a writer describes something by calling it something else

classification: grouping things according to similarities

taciturn: habitually untalkative; laconic; uncommunicative

Literacy Skill: Reasoning

Analyzing Graphs and Charts Across the Curriculum

Overview

This training script was the first one that our Restructuring Committee developed and implemented to support our Reasoning literacy skill. It was also intended to support our math department with a school wide initiative. We had experienced significant improvement in the ELA MCAS because of our school wide open response writing initiative, and we felt by focusing the entire school on graphing, we would help our students improve on the math MCAS. This literacy workshop first teaches the faculty the characteristics of bar graphs, circle graphs, circle/pie charts, and line graphs, and then instructs the teachers in how to model for their students a process to analyze, interpret and create graphs, tables, and charts. You will notice that in the workshop we have faculty practicing the skill. The samples we selected for the faculty include graphs and charts from a variety of content areas to demonstrate how this skill can be incorporated in all classes. Once the faculty was trained, teachers were then instructed to utilize graphs, tables, or charts in their own content area and implement the lesson with their students according to a calendar of implementation. So students were introduced to this process for analyzing and creating graphs and charts, and then practiced it repeatedly throughout the year in all content areas. The steps included in the routine are aligned with the expectations set by the Common Core State Standards listed below. These steps support students as they discern important information, interpret data, draw conclusions, and generate responses. It also demonstrates for all teachers how to incorporate the teaching of this important reasoning skill across the curriculum. Just as with our school wide writing initiative, this graphing initiative reinforced our commitment to teaching important skills and thinking routines across the curriculum.

Faculty Training Script

Analyzing Graphs and Charts Across the Curriculum

Literacy Skills: Reasoning
Lesson Duration: 50 minutes
Link to Common Core State Standards
- **CCSS.ELA-Literacy.CCRA.R.7** Integrate and evaluate content presented in diverse media and formats, including visually and quantitatively, as well as in words.
- **CCSS.ELA-Literacy.Reading for Sci/Tech. 7** Translate quantitative or technical information expressed in words in a text into visual form (e.g., a table or chart) and translate information expressed visually or mathematically (e.g., in an equation) into words.

Learning Outcomes:
As a result of this training, faculty will be able to:
- Implement the reasoning skills: to create, interpret, and explain a table, chart, or graph; to read, breakdown, and solve a word problem; to identify a pattern, explain a pattern, and/or make a prediction based on a pattern; to explain the logic of an argument or a solution.
- Implement the reading skill: to understand a concept and construct meaning.
- Model the steps for reading and analyzing a chart or graph for students.
- Instruct their students in the reading and analyzing graphs and charts process using guided practice and independent practice.
- Apply the steps of reading and analyzing charts and graphs to their content area
- Interpret and evaluate content as it relates to the graphics and charts used.
- Assess the students' work using the Graphing Rubric.

I. Introduction

Today's session will focus on helping students analyze graphs and charts across the curriculum. When we analyzed the Spring MCAS questions, we found that numerous problems asked our students to demonstrate high level graphing skills. In fact, seven graphing questions equaled 18 percent of the total math test. While we may typically think of graphs and charts in terms of math, these visuals are actually more about critical thinking and reasoning. Developing graphing activities in all classes better prepares students for both the MCAS test and real-life experiences in which students are asked to solve problems by interpreting and evaluating visual data.

Today we will work toward using a common vocabulary and process to help students analyze, develop, and apply graphs across all disciplines. Refer to your Graph Vocabulary handout as we first review the types of graphs and then explore the process of developing and applying graphs to solve problems. Let's begin by reviewing the main three types of graphs: bar graphs, pie/circle graphs, and line graphs.

II. Teaching the Strategy

Bar Graph
A bar graph is a visual display used to compare the amounts or frequency of occurrence of different characteristics of data. This type of display allows us to compare groups of data and make generalizations about the data quickly.

Point out the parts of the bar graph as you review them.

When reading a bar graph, carefully review these parts.

- *Graph title—The graph title gives an overview of the information being presented in the graph. The title is given at the top of the graph.*
- *Axes and their labels—Each graph has two axes. The axes labels tell us what information is presented on each axis. One axis represents data groups; the other axis represents the amounts or frequency of data groups.*
- *Grouped data axis—The grouped data axis is always at the base of the bars. This axis displays the type of data being graphed.*
- *Frequency data axis—The frequency axis has a scale that is a measure of the frequency or amounts of the different data groups.*

- **Axes scale**—*Scale is the range of values being presented along the frequency axis.*
- **Bars**—*The bars are rectangular blocks that can have their base at either vertical axis or horizontal axis (as in this example). Each bar represents the data for one of the data groups.*

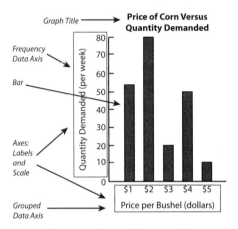

Use the following steps when reading a bar graph.
- **Step 1:** *Read the title and write what the graph is describing in your own words.*
- **Step 2:** *Explain what is being described by each axis. Find the label and the unit of measure on the horizontal axis and on the vertical axis. Determine the relationship between the axes. If the label or unit of measurement is not apparent, use the information in the title and/or any descriptions provided to determine this information. If the problem provided has no numbers on the vertical axis, find and label the axis.*
- **Step 3:** *Identify data points (tops of bars).*
- **Step 4:** *Create your own questions related to the graph.*

Pie Graph/Circle Graphs
A pie graph, also called a circle graph, is another tool by which we compare data. This graph is used when comparing the parts of a whole. A pie graph is cut up into pieces and addresses percentages in either a percent or fractional form: the bigger the piece of the pie graph, the larger the part of the whole that category encompasses. A pie graph emphasizes estimation; since each sector is proportional in size, we can easily make generalizations and comparisons.

Point out the parts of the pie graph as you review them. *When reading a pie/circle graph, carefully review these parts.*
- *Graph title: A graph title gives an overview of the information displayed in the graph. The title is given at the top of the graph.*
- *Sectors: Each sector represents one part of the whole. The size of each sector represents its fraction of the whole.*
- *Sector labels: The label of each sector indicates the category of information it refers to and may also give numeric data (often a percentage), so we know the size of each sector.*

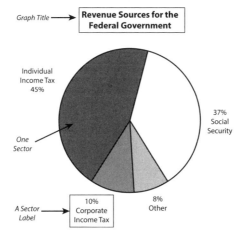

Use the following steps when reading a pie/circle graph.
- *Step 1: Read the title and write what the graph is describing in your own words.*
- *Step 2: Explain what is being described by each sector and the relationship between sectors. Find the label and the unit of measure on the graph. If the label or unit of measurement is not apparent, use the information in the title and/or any descriptions provided to determine this information.*
- *Step 3: Identify sector values or percentages.*
- *Step 4: Create your own questions related to the graph.*

Line Graph
Line graphs compare two variables, and each variable is plotted along an axis. Line graphs are useful for showing specific values of data, meaning that given one variable the other can easily be determined.

Point out the parts of the line graph as you review them. *When reading a line graph, carefully review these parts:*
- *Graph Title: As with the other types of graphs, the title is usually at the top.*
- *Horizontal axis (or X-Axis): This line on the graph is parallel to the horizon and moves left to right. This line usually represents time.*
- *Vertical axis (or Y-Axis): This line on the graph is perpendicular to the horizon and moves up and down. It usually shows what is happening over time.*
- *Data point: This point on the graph is where the coordinates of the X and Y axes intersect to provide a piece of data. The data point reflects the relationship between the X and Y axes named by the coordinates.*

Line graphs show trends and changes in data clearly and illustrate how one variable is affected by the other as it increases or decreases. They also allow the viewer to make predictions about the results of data not yet recorded.

Unfortunately, it is possible to alter the way a line graph appears to make data look a certain way. This is done by either not using consistent scales on the axes, meaning that the value in between each point along the axis may not be the same, or by comparing two graphs that use different scales. Be aware that the look of the data on the graph might not be the way the data really is.

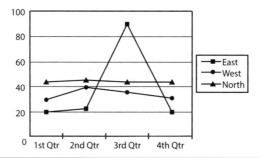

Use the following steps when reading a line graph.
- **Step 1:** Read the title and write what a graph is describing in your own words.
- **Step 2:** Explain what is being described by each axis, and determine the relationship between axes. Find the label and the unit of measure on the horizontal axis (x-axis) and on the vertical axis (y-axis). If the label or unit of measurement is not apparent, use the information in the title and/or any descriptions provided to determine this information.
- **Step 3:** Mark data points with visible dots. These dots can then be labeled as an ordered pair (x-value, y-value).
- **Step 4:** Create your own questions related to the graph.

III. Modeling the Strategy

Now that we understand the vocabulary and the four steps in analyzing charts and graphs, let's go through some examples.

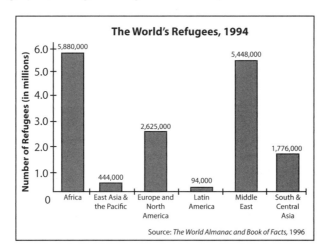

Step 1: First I read the title and write what the graph is describing. In this case, I may write, "The graph shows the number of the world's refugees in 1994."

Step 2: Then I explain what is being described by each axis by finding the label and the unit of measure on the horizontal axis and vertical axis. For example, I may write, "The horizontal, or x-axis, shows various regions of the world. The vertical, or y-axis, shows the number of refugees in millions."

Step 3: Next I identify the data points. The data points are the tops of the bars. In this graph they have been identified, but you could ask students to identify what the data points mean. For example, I may write, "In 1994 Africa had 5,880,000 refugees."

Step 4: The final step is to create my own questions related to the graph. On an assessment, these may be given to the student. Some examples are as follows:
1. What is the subject of this chart?
2. Which world region has the most refugees? The fewest?
3. How many of the world's refugees are from the Middle East? From East Asia and the Pacific?
4. The total number of refugees in 1994 was 16,267,000. You can calculate the percentage of refugees from each region by dividing the number of refugees from a region by the total number of refugees for 1994. For example, there were 5,880,000 refugees in Africa in 1994. If you divide 5,880,000 by 16,267,000, you will find that 36 percent of the world's refugees were from Africa. Calculate the number of refugees from each of the other world regions.
5. What conclusion can you reach concerning the large number of refugees from Africa and the Middle East versus the small number from East Asia and Latin America?

Note that questions 1 through 3 start out easy asking students to identify specific information on the graph. Questions 4 and 5 require students to demonstrate higher level skills. Question 4, requires students to interpret information and perform calculations. Since students are calculating percentages, this question could be raised to a higher level by asking students to create a pie or circle graph. Question 5 asks students to draw conclusions based on the analysis of information from the graph. You could expand this activity by adding additional questions or having students come up with complex questions that could be presented to the class.

Let's work through the process again using a pie graph.

**Revenue Sources for the
Federal Government**

Individual
Income Tax
45%

37%
Social
Security

10%
Corporate
Income Tax

8%
Other

Step 1: *First I write what the chart is describing: "The pie graph describes the sources from which the government receives money."*

Step 2: *Next I describe each sector: "The graph contains four different sectors, meaning the graph displays four different sources of revenue. The largest sector—Individual Income Tax, is a little less than half of the whole circle. Social Security is another sector that is also relatively large. Corporate Income Tax and Other are two smaller sectors."*

Step 3: *Next I identify sector values or percentages. "The largest sector, 45 percent of the total revenue, comes from individual income tax. The smallest sector, 8 percent, comes from sources listed as other. Individual income tax provides four and a half times as much income as corporate income tax. Social security is the second largest source of revenue at 37 percent."*

Step 4: *Finally I write my own questions related to the graph. With this particular graph, I might have students ask questions about the relationship of the sectors. In addition, I could ask students to make predictions about budget cuts or recommend a solution to a revenue problem using the pie graph.*

IV. Assessment

Now that we have practiced the four steps, let's use the following example to work through the process in small groups. When you get to step 4, answer the questions I have posted.

Post the following description, line graph, and questions for teachers to see.

In a few years, you might be interested in getting some kind of part-time job. You find the following line graph, which plots the minimum wage versus time from October 1938 to June 2009. What kinds of things might you be able to tell from it?

The Federal Hourly Minimum Wage Since Its Inception

Source: United States Department of Labor

1. What was the minimum wage in January 1978?
2. When did the minimum wage reach $3.35?
3. In which years did the largest increase in the minimum wage occur?
4. Based on your observations of the graph, make a prediction about what the wage might be in the year 2015.
5. What about the scales used on the graph might make the data appear differently than how it really is?

Allow small groups time to work through the process and then reconvene the whole group to work through any problems or answer any questions.

Answers:
1. The minimum wage in January 1978 reached $ 2.65. This could be determined by finding January 1978 on the *x*-axis and following it up until you hit the line.
2. The minimum wage reached $3.35 in January 1981. This answer could be reached by finding $3.35 on the line and following it down until you hit the *x*-axis.
3. The largest increase shown on the graph is $0.70, which happened three times: in 2007 (from $5.15 to $5.85), 2008 (from $5.85 to $6.55), and 2009 (from $6.55 to $7.25).
4. This is a tricky question because the time periods in between each increase are different. Because of this, there is not a constant rate at which the minimum wage increases. It is possible that the wage would not increase at all by 2015. If it did increase, one way to judge how much would be recent increases. The five latest increases (Oct. 1996–July 2009) averaged $0.60 each. Therefore, a good guess based on this graph would be that the minimum wage in 2015 might increase from $7.25 to $7.85 or $8.45.
5. If you looked carefully at the *x*-axis, you would see that even though each time period is marked an equal distance apart, they are not really consistent time differences. For instance, the graph goes from April 1990 to April 1991 to October 1996. Obviously there is one year between the first two while there are over five years between the second two. This inconsistency makes the data appear differently than how it really is.

While we have mostly analyzed graphs today, let's look at an activity that asks students to use their reading comprehension skills, apply their knowledge of graphs to create one of their own, and synthesize information from text and graphs to solve a problem. This type of authentic activity can raise rigor and relevance in our classrooms.

Provide teachers with a copy of the activity. Review the handout together, and answer any questions teachers may have about how graphs have been used in this activity.

Handout

Activity: The Marketing of a CD

Name _____ Date _____

Cost of a CD

A typical music fan who buys a CD might use that CD at home, take that CD in the car, make another CD of that CD, or using it as part of a compilation, play that CD with friends and for friends, keep it for many years. That's probably why most consumers describe CDs as a good value. At the same time, when asked directly whether CDs cost too much, some consumers will say yes! *Why the contradiction?* Because some consumers don't understand why the sales tag on a CD is so much higher than the cost of producing the actual physical disc—a cost, which in fact, has decreased over the years.

While the RIAA (Recording Industry Association of America) does not collect information on the specific costs that make up the price of a CD, there are many factors that go into the overall cost of a CD. The plastic it's pressed on is among the least significant. CD manufacturing costs may be lower, but it takes more money than ever before to put out a new recording.

Of course, the most important component of a CD is the artist's effort in developing that music. Artists spend a large portion of their creative energy on writing song lyrics and composing music or working with producers and A&R executives to find great songs from great writers. This task can take weeks, months, or even years. The creative ability of these artists to produce the music we love, combined with the time and energy they spend throughout that process is in itself priceless. But while the creative process is priceless, it must be compensated. Artists receive royalties on each recording, which vary according to their contract, and the songwriter gets royalties too. In addition, the label incurs additional costs in finding and signing new artists.

Once an artist or group has songs composed, they must then go into the studio and begin recording. The costs of recording this work, including recording studio fees, studio musicians, sound engineers, producers and others, all must be recovered by the cost of the CD.

Then comes the marketing and promotional costs—perhaps the most expensive part of the music business today. They include increasingly expensive video clips, public relations, tour support, marketing campaigns, and promotion to get the songs played on the radio. For example, when you hear a song played on the radio, that didn't just happen! Labels make investments in artists by paying for both the production and the promotion of the album, and promotion is very expensive. New technology, such as the Internet, offers new ways for artists to reach music fans, but it still requires that some entity, whether a traditional label or another kind of company, markets and promotes that artist so that fans are aware of new releases.

For every album released in a given year, a marketing strategy is developed to make that album stand out among the other releases that hit the market that year. Art must be designed for the CD box, and promotional materials (posters, store displays, and music videos) must be developed and produced. For many artists, a costly concert tour is essential to promote their recordings.

Another factor commonly overlooked in assessing CD prices is assuming that all CDs are equally profitable. In fact, the vast majority are never profitable. After production, recording, promotional, and distribution costs, most never sell enough to recover these costs, let alone make a profit. In the end, less than 10 percent are profitable, and in effect, these recordings finance all the rest.

Clearly there are many costs associated with producing a CD, and despite these costs, the price of recorded music to consumers has fallen dramatically since CDs were first introduced in 1983. Between 1983 and 1996, the average price of a CD fell by more than 40 percent. Over this same period of time, consumer prices (measured by the Consumer Price Index, or CPI) rose nearly 60 percent. If CD prices had risen at the same rate as consumer prices over this period, the average retail price of a CD in 1996 would have been $33.86 instead of $12.75. While the price of CDs has fallen, the amount of music provided on a typical CD has increased substantially, along with the quality in terms of fidelity, durability, ease of use, and range of extras (e.g., music videos, interviews and discographies). Content of this type often requires considerable production expense and adds a whole new dimension that goes beyond conventional audio.

In contrast, CD prices are low compared to other forms of entertainment. CDs are one of the few entertainment units to decrease in price, even though production, marketing, and distribution costs have increased. In a *USA Today* article entitled "Spending a Fortune for Fun," a reporter observes, "The cost of entertainment is rising along with our willingness to pay it. Though some factions of the industry see price resistance—CD prices are relatively low and home videos rentals are still a bargain— consumers don't seem to balk at the rising price of fun in this strong, family-friendly economy." The prices of other forms of entertainment have risen, on average, more rapidly than has music or consumer prices, with most admission prices for other forms of entertainment having increased more than 90 percent between 1983 and 1996.

By all measures, when you consider how long people have the music and how often they can go back and get "re-entertained," CDs truly are an incredible value for the money.

The table below represents retail dollar sales (in millions of dollars):

	2002	2003	2004	2005
Music CDs	803.0	746.0	767.0	705.5

1. Create an appropriate graph below to display the data in the table above. Supply an appropriate title, *y*-axis label, and *x*-axis label.

Sample answer for graph

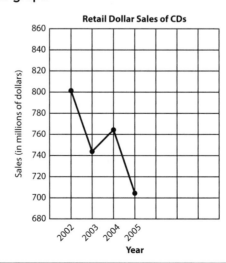

2. From the reading passage above and your own knowledge about music CDs, cite some reasons why sales are projected to decrease.
3. As cited in the article above, "assessing CD prices [assumes] that all CDs are equally profitable. In fact, the vast majority are never profitable. After production, recording, promotional, and distribution costs, most never sell enough to recover these costs, let alone make a profit. In the end, less than 10 percent are profitable, and in effect, these recordings finance all the rest."

It is estimated that over the last five years, the costs associated with producing a CD have risen 60 percent. If the average price of a music CD was $12.95 five years ago and the costs associated with producing a CD were factored in, what should be the approximate price of a CD today? Show your work.

4. Discuss the reasons why you think the cost of CDs reflect (or do not reflect) the price you calculated above. Use examples from your graph and/or the reading passage.

V. Summary

Helping our students become more proficient with reading, interpreting, and creating charts and graphs across the curriculum means preparing them for their lives beyond the school walls. Using the four-step process consistently and repeatedly, we can build their confidence in analyzing visuals while also strengthening their problem solving and reasoning skills. Graphs and charts can communicate ideas powerfully in all disciplines, and working together we can encourage our students to unlock their meaning and potential.

Graphing Activity Rubric		
Name:	**Date:**	
Labels and Titles	**Numerical Correctness**	**Visual Presentation**
4 Points • Graph is titled appropriately. • Graph is labeled correctly and appropriately placed. • Answers to interpretive questions are labeled with correct units.	**8 Points** • Numerical data is placed correctly on the graph. • Graph scaled appropriately (no awkward jumps in values). • Answers to interpretive questions are correct and complete.	
3 Points • Graph is titled appropriately. • Most labels are correct and placed appropriately. • Answers to interpretive questions are labeled with correct units in most cases.	**6 Points** • Numerical data is placed on the graph correctly in most cases. • Graph scaled appropriately (no awkward jumps in values). • Answers to interpretive questions are mostly correct and complete.	**2 Points** • Graph is neat and legible. • Reader is able to find values by looking at the graph. • Interpretive questions are written neatly and in complete sentences.
2 Points • Graph is not titled. • Some labels are correct and appropriately placed. • Interpretive questions are labeled with correct units in some cases.	**4 Points** • Numerical data is placed on the graph correctly in some cases. • Graph scaling is attempted. • Answers to some interpretive questions are correct and complete.	

1 Point	**2 Points**	**1 Point**
• Graph is not titled. • Most labels are incorrectly or inappropriately placed. • Interpretive questions are labeled with incorrect units in the majority of cases.	• Numerical data is placed on the graph incorrectly in most cases. • Graph scaled incorrectly. • Answers to most interpretive questions are incorrect and incomplete.	• Neatness and legibility are lacking, but the graph is readable. • Reader will have some difficulty finding values on the graph. • Answers to interpretive questions need to be neater and complete sentences must be written.
0 Points Graph is not titled. • Labels are not present. • No units are given with answers on interpretive questions.	**0 Points** • No data placed on graph. • Graph not scaled at all. • Answers to interpretive questions entirely incorrect or missing	

Evaluated by (circle one):	Self	Peer	Teacher

Scoring:
   • **13–14 = Advanced**
   • **11–12 = Proficient**
   • **8–10 = Needs Improvement**
   • **0–7 = Failing**
	Total Score

Comments:

Graphing Vocabulary

Average (mean)—a number that is representative of a set of data (e.g. the average daily temperature). The average is found by adding each element of the data and dividing by the number of elements.

Bar—a shaded rectangle representing the relationship between the **x-axis** and the **y-axis** on a **bar graph**. The end segment (or the end of the **bar**) represents the **data point**.

Bar graph—a type of graph that shows results that are one time, or not continuous. Independent pieces of information are provided (e.g., the results of a survey).

Circle graph/Pie graph—used to compare the parts of a whole.

Coordinates—the individual **values** on the **x-** and **y-axes**.

Data point—the point on a **graph** where the **coordinates** of the **x-** and **y-axes** intersect to provide a piece of data. The **data point** reflects the relationship between the **x-** and **y-axes** named by the **coordinates**.

Factual—true and accurate information provided on the **graph**.

Graph—a visual representation of a relationship between two quantities that are called variables.

Horizontal axis (or **x-axis**)—the line on the graph that is parallel (i.e., two lines that do not intersect) to the horizon. This line moves left to right.

Inference—a conclusion that is drawn from the **factual** information provided by the graph.

Label—identifies the quantity, item, or element being measured on each **axis** of a **graph**.

Line graph—a type of **graph** that is used to show trends and changes, for example, economic changes (indicating a growth or a decline).

Ordered pair—names a **data point**. The **x-coordinate** is named first, followed by the **y-coordinate**, separated by a comma and enclosed in parentheses (x, y).

Percent—a ratio that compares a number to 100.

Rectangle—a parallelogram (a four-sided figure with two pairs of parallel sides) with four right angles.

Sector—a section of a **circle graph/pie graph**.

Trend—a direction of movement between **data points** indicated by the connecting lines.

Unit of measurement—one measure specified on an axis of a graph in equal increments (e.g., inches, miles, gallons, dollars, etc.).

Value—an assigned quantity, item or element indicated on each **axis** of a **graph**.

Vertical axis (or **y-axis**)—the line on the **graph** that is perpendicular (i.e., at right angles) to the horizon. This line moves up and down.

X-axis—the horizontal line that represents one component of the **graph** (often represents time).

Y-axis—the vertical line that represents one component of the **graph.**

Literacy Skill: Speaking

Developing Student Speaking Skills

Overview

This literacy workshop is not about test performance. It was developed as a direct response to a strong request from the faculty based on their concern that our students were not presenting themselves well. Their writing skills had improved dramatically, but we had not yet tackled their speaking skills. It was also developed to provide our teachers with more tools to engage the students in class discussions. This training script focuses on activities designed to generate high-quality discussions with students. The strategies included in this training align with expectations set by the Common Core State Standards listed below. Using these strategies, faculty can build discussions in which all students participate and learn. In addition, in order to assess oral presentations, the Restructuring Committee has developed and included an oral presentation rubric. These are strategies that can and should be used in every content area to encourage and promote student participation.

Faculty Training Script

Developing Student Speaking Skills
Literacy Skill: Writing **Lesson Duration:** 50 minutes **Link to Common Core State Standards:** • **CCSS.ELA-Literacy.CCRA.SL.1** Prepare for and participate effectively in a range of conversations and collaborations with diverse partners, building on others' ideas and expressing their own clearly and persuasively. • **CCSS.ELA-Literacy.CCRA.SL.2** Integrate and evaluate information presented in diverse media and formats, including visually, quantitatively, and orally. • **CCSS.ELA-Literacy.CCRA.SL.3** Evaluate a speaker's point of view, reasoning, and use of evidence and rhetoric.

- **CCSS.ELA-Literacy.CCRA.SL.4** Present information, findings, and supporting evidence such that listeners can follow the line of reasoning and the organization, development, and style are appropriate to task, purpose, and audience.
- **CCSS.ELA-Literacy.CCRA.SL.5** Make strategic use of digital media and visual displays of data to express information and enhance understanding of presentations.
- **CCSS.ELA-Literacy.CCRA.SL.6** Adapt speech to a variety of contexts and communicative tasks, demonstrating command of formal English when indicated or appropriate.

Learning Outcomes

As a result of this training, faculty will be able to:

- Implement the speaking literacy skills: to convey one's thinking in complete sentences; to participate in a class discussion or a public forum; to make an oral presentation to one's class, one's peers, or one's community; to communicate in a manner that allows one to be both heard and understood.
- Individually complete the warm up sheet on obstacles.
- Have small group/pair discussions in inner/outer circle on obstacles and ways to overcome these obstacles.
- Create a chart/overhead in small groups to reach consensus (refined answers).
- Use all these discussion strategies in classes whenever appropriate.
- Discuss the rubric for oral presentations in whole-group discussion.
- Utilize the oral presentation rubric in class to assess students' presentations.

I. Introduction

Welcome to the student-speaking skills training focused on engaging students in high-quality discussions for learning.

After today you will be able to set up and implement class discussions that lead to all students participating and learning. We will discuss three strategies to help achieve this: four-corners activity, inner-outer circle, and full-class discussion. You will also be able to use/modify an oral presentation rubric that defines expectations and awards points for both speaking skills and content.

Take a few moments to reflect on the following questions.
- What difficulties have you experienced or anticipate experiencing when arranging an oral presentation by a student or small group?
- What difficulties have you experienced or anticipate experiencing when arranging a whole-class discussion?
- What could you do to prevent these difficulties and get the best learning experience out of class discussion or presentations?

Allow faculty members one to two minutes to reflect and then have volunteers share some of their thoughts.

Today we will focus on three strategies that may overcome some of the obstacles you have experienced when engaging students in oral presentations and/or class discussions.

II. Teaching the Strategy

The following strategies increase the quality of student discussion. We will use each strategy to discuss further your experiences and obstacles with oral presentations and class discussions.

Strategy 1: Four-Corners Activity (10–15 minutes)

The first strategy is the four-corners activity. Use this activity to help students generate and share their ideas.

Use these steps to implement the four-corners activity:
1. *After students have individually written their response to a question, divide the class into four groups.*
2. *Give each group a large sheet of paper and a marker to record their ideas. Choose a recorder and a spokesperson.*
3. *Give groups ten minutes or so to generate their answers.*
4. *Have everyone return to their seats. Post the four sheets on the board and ask each spokesperson to come up to review his or her group's ideas.*
5. *Others in the audience have the responsibility of taking notes.*

Now let's use this activity to answer the following question: What do you see as obstacles to conducting class discussions?

Follow the steps of the activity with the faculty.

Strategy 2: Inner Circle/Outer Circle Activity (15–20 minutes)

The next strategy is the inner circle/outer circle activity. This activity gets all students actively speaking and listening about a question or topic.

Use these steps to implement the inner circle/outer circle activity:
1. *Allow students time to respond to a question or topic in a written response.*
2. *Place half of the students in the inner circle and the remaining half in a circle surrounding them.*
3. *Have the inner circle speak for five minutes on Question 1. Outer circle people jot notes, comments, and questions. Then open up discussion to include the outer circle for two more minutes. Please note that the ideal number for the inner circle is four to five students; however, for our purposes today, we may increase that number.*
4. *Have the outer circle exchange seats with the inner circle to speak for five minutes on Question 2. The outer circle people jot notes, comments, and questions; after five minutes they may be included in the discussion for two more minutes.*

Now let's use this activity to answer the following questions:
1. *How do you deal with the issue of the shy/reluctant speaker in your class?*
2. *What are students in the audience being asked to do during individual or group presentations to the class?*

Follow the steps of the activity with the faculty.

Strategy 3: Full-Class Discussion (10–15 minutes)

A strategy that you have probably used is full-class discussion. However, effectively configuring the room and setting guidelines can greatly improve the quality of full-class discussion.

Use these steps to implement a full-class discussion:
1. *Allow students time to write a response to a question or topic.*
2. *Configure the room so that participants are facing each other.*
3. *Set guidelines such as raising hands, speaking in complete sentences, or responding to the previous speaker (e.g., "I agree," "I disagree," "I would like to add…").*

Now let's use this activity to answer the following questions:
1. *What criteria do you use for grading class discussions?*
2. *What criteria might you use for grading the four-corners activity? The inner circle/outer circle activity? The full-class discussion?*

Follow the steps of the activity with the faculty.

Please note that in all speaking activities, you may find that using a class list is helpful for grading purposes.

III. Assessment

The Restructuring Committee continues to discuss and plan for the implementation of our literacy objectives. At the end of last year, a discussion regarding the level of speaking skills of our students resulted in an overall sense of dissatisfaction. The committee was concerned with how our students often presented themselves in classes, even when they were making formal, planned presentations. In response to this discussion, the Restructuring Committee developed a rubric for oral presentations that attempts to meld the quality of presentation with the delivery of content. This also supports a recommendation presented by our Visiting Team for Accreditation regarding the need to develop schoolwide rubrics. We think this rubric addresses a serious need.

Review the rubric with faculty. Point out the different sections of the rubric and elaborate as necessary.
1. *Under the category of SPEAKING SKILLS, the committee selected the following criteria for assessment: delivery, eye contact, posture, and volume.*
2. *Under the category of CONTENT, the Committee tried to mirror from the Collins Writing program.*
   - *The student presents his or her thesis in a clear **introduction**.*
   - ***Topic development** includes all elements previously determined by the teacher in the assignment. For example, you may insist that students use certain vocabulary words or a particular number of specific examples. In other words, this category refers specifically to the requirements in the assignment directions. Also included is an assessment of the presentation organization and the speaker's understanding of the material.*

- In the **conclusion,** presenters should highlight their key ideas and conclude with a strong final statement. They should also be able to field questions from the teacher or classroom audience, if appropriate. Please note that fielding questions may provide the opportunity to give credit to those students who participate by asking good questions. This may help deter a lack of attention or participation on the part of audience members.

Suggestions for using this oral presentation rubric include having students grade each other, assessing individual or group presentations, and having presenters self-evaluate.

IV. Summary

Please note that this oral presentation rubric is a work in progress. As you incorporate oral presentations and discussions into your classes, please try this rubric and provide any feedback, positive or negative, to your department head who will forward comments to the Administrative Team and Restructuring Committee. Just as with the rubric for assessing open responses, we want to improve this tool to make it as helpful as possible for every teacher.

You can begin to use the three activities—four-corners activity, inner circle/outer circle activity, and full-class discussion—to raise the quality of discussions in your classroom and improve student learning.

Oral Presentation Rubric

Presenter: _____ Evaluator: _____

Literacy in Speaking:
- to make an oral presentation to one's class
- to communicate in a manner that allows one to be both heard and understood
- to convey one's thinking in complete sentences

SPEAKING SKILLS	All Elements Present	Most Elements Present	Some Elements Present	No Elements Present
Delivery Presenter doesn't rush, shows enthusiasm, avoids *like, um, kind of, you know,* etc. Uses complete sentences.	4	3	2	1
Eye Contact Presenter keeps head up, does not read, and speaks to whole audience.	4	3	2	1
Posture Presenter stands up straight, faces audience, and doesn't fidget.	4	3	2	1
Volume Presenter can be easily heard by all. No gum chewing, etc.	4	3	2	1

CONTENT	All Elements Present	Most Elements Present	Some Elements Present	No Elements Present
Introduction Presentation begins with a clear focus/ thesis.	4	3	2	1
Topic Development A Presentation includes all elements previously determined by the teacher.	4	3	2	1
Topic Development B Presentation is clearly organized. Material is logically sequenced, related to thesis, and not repetitive.	4	3	2	1
Topic Development C Presentation shows full grasp and understanding of the material.	4	3	2	1
Conclusion A Presentation highlights key ideas and concludes with a strong final statement.	4	3	2	1
Conclusion B Presenter fields questions easily.	4	3	2	1

Total Number of Points:
35–40 = A   29–34 = B   23–28 = C   17–22 = D   10–16 = F

* Evaluator: Place comments beside each descriptor

Literacy Skill: Reasoning

Problem-Solving Strategies Across the Content Areas

Overview

This training script was developed after we reviewed the math MCAS exam and saw many questions that involved problem solving. Many problems on the MCAS include multiple parts to the question. Students have to read the question carefully and work through the problem presented. An examination of our data demonstrated that our students were struggling with these types of questions. They were not displaying thinking routines and problem-solving strategies to help them work their way through the problem and come up with a solution.

The Restructuring Committee developed this literacy workshop to teach the faculty how to prepare their students to attack these types of questions. To implement problem-solving strategies across the curriculum we focused the workshop on four problem-solving strategies which could be used across all content areas: systematic lists, drawing a diagram, working backward, and eliminating the possibilities. The steps and routines associated with these problem-solving strategies are aligned with the expectations set by the Common Core State Standard listed below. These strategies help students think logically about a problem, develop a plan, and communicate a possible solution; they are tools students can use in all aspects of their lives. It also demonstrated to our teachers that every discipline can help develop thinking routines that can be used in the math and science areas and teachers can utilize those strategies in their classes with their students.

Faculty Training Script

Problem-Solving Strategies Across the Content Areas

Literacy Skill: Reasoning
Lesson Duration: 50 minutes
Link to Common Core State Standards:

- **CCSS.Math.Practice.MP1** Make sense of problems and persevere in solving them.

Learning Outcomes:
As a result of this training, faculty will be able to:

- Read, break down, and solve a word problem.
- Identify a pattern, explain a pattern, and/or make a prediction based on a pattern.
- Detect a fallacy in an argument or proof.
- Explain the logic of an argument or solution.
- Use analogies or evidence to support one's thinking.

I. Introduction

Welcome to the problem-solving strategies training. Once we identify skills our students need to practice, we provide them with specific strategies to practice and learn in order to successfully negotiate the skills. Our goal with this training is to "attack" problem solving and provide our students with strategies that can help them determine ways to solve a problem.

In this training we will introduce four important problem-solving strategies that you can teach to students as well as a problem-solving rubric. The four strategies are applicable in all content areas. In our follow-up faculty workshop in two weeks, we will meet in departments to discuss how these strategies best fit within each content area.

II. Teaching the Strategy

What is problem solving? **Allow a few teachers to answer.** *Problem solving has been defined as what to do when you don't know what to do. We problem-solve every day, but it doesn't involve solving math problems or using equations. We use a logical thought process and then communicate the plan.*

By giving our students these strategies, we increase their confidence. Even when they can't immediately solve the problem, they will persist and develop an attack plan. They don't have to be a math whiz to do this. Teachers in every content area play a vital role in teaching students how to apply these strategies. These are not just math problems—they are critical thinking problems.

Next, introduce the four problem-solving strategies as described below. (The strategies are from Johnson, K. and Herr, T. (2001). *Crossing the river with dogs: Problem solving strategies.* **Key Curriculum Press.)**

Strategy 1: Systematic Lists

A systematic list is a strategy particularly useful when generating a list of possible outcomes. A system is any procedure that allows you to do something (like organize information) in a methodical way. The method used in a systematic list should be understandable and clear so that the person making the list can verify its accuracy quickly.

While many people make lists, they often don't identify or recognize the method they are using to make the list. In this strategy, clearly identifying and using the system is the key. It's the difference between making a grocery list at random and organizing the same list by types of food or the layout of a particular store. This method ensures a more accurate and complete list, giving information a structure that allows the brain to more easily absorb and interpret the information. Patterns emerge from a systematic list, and it becomes more of a learning tool. Note the difference between the random grocery list and the systemic list depicted:

Random Grocery List		Systematic Grocery List	
Eggs	Oranges	*Produce/Fruit*	*Condiments*
Milk	Red Peppers	Oranges	Pickles
Yogurt	Toilet Paper	Apples	Relish
Peas	English Muffins	Grapes	
Chicken	Broccoli		*Paper Goods*
American	Turkey Breast	*Produce/*	Toilet Paper
Cheese	Relish	*Vegetables*	Napkins
Pickles	Napkins	Peas	
Cheerios	Corn	Broccoli	*Deli*
Pretzels		Red Peppers	Turkey Breast
		Corn	
			Dairy
		Meat	Yogurt
		Chicken	Milk
			Eggs
		Cereal	
		Cheerios	*Grains/Bread*
			English Muffins

Use the following steps when using systematic lists to problem-solve:

1. *Actively read the question or problem.*
2. *Break down the problem and determine what the problem is asking.*
3. *Restate the problem in your own words.*
4. *Organize the information into a systematic list that will help solve the problem asked. For example, your list can be in categories or represent patterns. In other words, your job is to determine a system of organization that will help you reach a conclusion or solution.*
5. *Follow your organizational strategy all the way through to ensure a complete systematic list.*
6. *Review the completed list to make sure all possibilities are included.*
7. *If you find that your strategy does not work, choose another systematic list or a different problem-solving strategy such as drawing a diagram, working backward, or eliminating the possibilities.*

Strategy 2: Drawing a Diagram

Drawing a diagram is a strategy particularly useful when you have a complicated word problem to solve. Often you can simplify complicated word problems by creating a visual representation. You've used diagrams like graphic organizers, tables, pictures, charts, graphs, and timelines in the past. Diagrams are a visual way to organize information and see relationships you might not otherwise see. One of the best examples of a diagram in the professional world is a blueprint. An architect's blueprint expresses ideas concisely in a visual form that leaves little to interpretation. A blueprint illustrates one of a diagram's strengths: the ability to present the whole picture immediately without the use of words. However, you can use words in diagrams in many ways to help visualize a solution to a question or problem.

In science, we might compare the characteristics of prokaryotic and eukaryotic cells. This relationship could be illustrated in a Venn diagram.

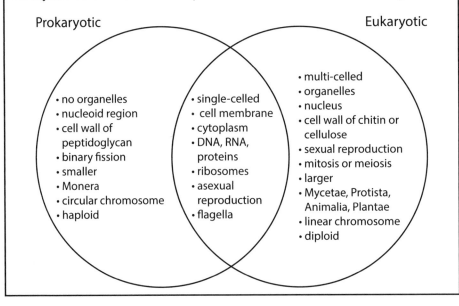

Prokaryotic

- no organelles
- nucleoid region
- cell wall of peptidoglycan
- binary fission
- smaller
- Monera
- circular chromosome
- haploid

- single-celled
- cell membrane
- cytoplasm
- DNA, RNA, proteins
- ribosomes
- asexual reproduction
- flagella

Eukaryotic

- multi-celled
- organelles
- nucleus
- cell wall of chitin or cellulose
- sexual reproduction
- mitosis or meiosis
- larger
- Mycetae, Protista, Animalia, Plantae
- linear chromosome
- diploid

Use the following steps when drawing a diagram to problem-solve:

1. *Actively read the question or problem.*
2. *Break down the problem and determine what the problem is asking.*
3. *Restate the problem in your own words.*
4. *Determine key information you need to arrive at a solution and use that information in steps 5 and 6.*
5. *Sketch a diagram that groups your key information <u>in a way that makes sense to you.</u> (Remember that a diagram can be in the form of graphic organizers, tables, pictures, charts, graphs, timelines, Venn diagrams, concept maps, etc.)*
6. *Manipulate the key information to find your answer. For example, draw lines, calculate, or shade areas of commonality.*
7. *If you find that your strategy does not work, choose another diagram or a different problem-solving strategy such as drawing, creating a systematic list, working backward, or eliminating the possibilities.*

Strategy 3: Working Backward
Working backward is a strategy particularly useful when you have the answer to a problem or a question but need to figure out what steps you took to get to the solution. Working backward is a way of changing focus. In working backward, you know the final answer but perform the opposite steps/functions in reverse order to find the starting point or missing information. One example is trying to develop a schedule for a particular event. If a wedding date is set for June, the couple must plan out details and deadlines for each task in order for everything to be ready by June. The couple may know that they need to mail invitations four to six weeks before the wedding, so they must also determine when to place the order for the invitations to allow for printing and delivery.

In another example, you might ask students to create a timeline that illustrates what led up to the outbreak of World War II in 1939 when Germany attacked Poland.

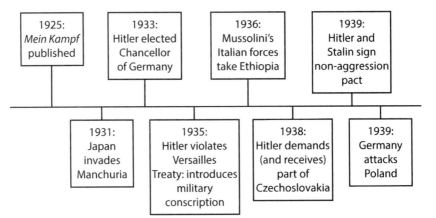

Use the following steps when working backward to problem-solve:
1. *Actively read the question or problem.*
2. *Break down the problem and determine what the problem is asking.*
3. *Restate the problem in your own words.*
4. *Identify the solution or end point presented in the problem.*
5. *Figure out what information is needed and/or missing to get to the end point or solution presented.*
6. *Organize the information in a way that makes sense or seems reasonable given the end point or solution. You might use other problem solving strategies such as systematic lists or drawing a diagram to do this.*
7. *Put the information together to make sure that it leads to the end point or solution presented.*

Strategy 4: Eliminate the Possibilities

The problem-solving strategy of eliminating possibilities is most useful when you are not necessarily looking for the right answer but rather looking at a lot of wrong answers. As each wrong answer is eliminated, you get closer to the right answer. This strategy is most commonly used with multiple-choice questions when a list of options is presented and one has to decide what choices will not work in answering the question. In many instances, eliminating the possibilities may lead to the best possible answer rather than the right answer. However, eliminating possibilities has many more applicable uses. The strategy is exemplified by playing the game Twenty Questions. For example:

- *The teacher selects an item in the room. The students ask yes-or-no questions to determine what the item is.*
- *The teacher may select the clock in the room. A student may begin the questioning by asking, "Is the object larger than a chair?"*
- *The teacher would respond, "No." Another student might ask, "Can the object move?" The teacher would respond, "Yes," and so on.*

Students need to be able to catalogue and remember the possibilities that have been eliminated in the effort to get to the correct response.

Use the following steps when eliminating possibilities to problem-solve:

1. *Actively read the question or problem.*
2. *Break down the problem and determine what the problem is asking.*
3. *Restate the problem in your own words.*
4. *Focus on what you know, not on what you don't know, and then generate a list of possible solutions to the problem.*
5. *Begin the elimination process by explaining why a presented solution will not work.*
6. *Justify why the solution you selected works best.*

III. Assessment

Problem Solving Rubric: The goal of introducing problem-solving strategies is to help students develop their ability to solve problems. This rubric recognizes that students have attempted to use one of the four introduced strategies to solve a problem and assesses how well they have used their reasoning skills.

	2	1	0	Student Score
Understanding the Problem	Shows complete understanding of the problem	Misinterprets part of the problem	Completely misinterprets the problem	
Choosing a Solution Strategy	Chooses a correct strategy that could lead to a correct solution if used without error	Chooses a strategy that could possibly lead to a correct solution, or chooses a strategy that will get him or her partway through the problem but fails to change strategies when appropriate; uses a correct strategy but fails to state the name of the strategy	Does not give evidence of using a strategy, or uses a totally inappropriate strategy	
Implementing the Strategy	Gets correct answer, states it, and labels it properly	Makes copying error or computational error, gets partial answer to a problem with multiple answers, or labels answer incorrectly	Gets no answer, fails to state the answer, or gets a wrong answer based on an appropriate solution strategy	
Explanation	Gives a clear, coherent, complete explanation	Gives an incomplete explanation, or the explanation is hard to follow	Makes no explanation or incoherent explanation	
			TOTAL	

Explain each section of the rubric.

  A. *Understanding the Problem:* Understanding (or misunderstanding) is generally conveyed to the teacher through the student's work, including the written explanation of the solution. Ideally the student is placing before you a comprehensive "map" of how he or she solved the problem. This "map" should also show you exactly where the students made turns, both right and wrong.

  B. *Choosing a Solution Strategy:* The student must also give the correct name of the strategy. You have to be careful here because a student may use a perfectly reasonable strategy that you had not thought to use. As you will see, there are many ways to solve a problem, and some problems have more than one equally good choice of strategy. Some problems require multiple strategies to solve the problem.

  C. *Implementing the Strategy:* Here the focus is on how well a student uses whatever strategy he or she picked. If the student chooses an appropriate strategy but doesn't apply it sensibly, he or she would get zero points here.

  D. *Getting the Answer:* The point is partly to make sure that the student gets the right answer. It is also to ensure that the student states the correct answer clearly since a student may sometimes give an answer to a question other than the one asked.

  E. *Explanation:* The student's explanation should be well thought out and well communicated "maps" of the reasoning he or she used to solve the problem. Not every detail is needed. Rather, the explanation is an organized, concise retelling of the thoughts, assumptions, and understanding that the student developed when solving the problem.

(from Crossing the River with Dogs: Problem Solving Strategies)

IV. Summary
Having students use the problem-solving strategies helps them become better thinkers. Remember the following when teaching these four strategies to your students: • *Model the strategy for students.* • *Emphasize to students that they may come to decision points at which a change in strategy or approach to solving the problem may be needed. In other words, while solving the problem one way, a student may realize that the problem is better or more easily solved another way with a different organizational strategy.* • *Stress that starting over may be helpful and necessary.* • *Make purposeful "mistakes" when modeling so that students can see how decisions are made to change an approach or change a strategy.*

Literacy Skill: Writing

Quickwrites

Overview

This training script focuses on developing students' writing abilities through the use of short, continual quickwrites. The intent of training teachers to use quickwrites in their classes was to continue to insist on writing across the curriculum, and to provide teachers with a tool for formative assessment. The implementation of this literacy skill differed from the implementation of the Open Response Writing process. With Open Response Writing, we used a calendar of implementation so that students were given deliberate, planned practice throughout the year to help them master the skill. For the quickwrites, there is no calendar of implementation. Rather, the intent is that teachers use quickwrites on a daily basis to develop students' writing skills and assess their learning. The steps included in quick writes correspond to the Common Core Standards included below. The steps support students incorporating elements of writing into every day and in every content area.

Faculty Training Script

<table>
<tr><td>Quickwrites</td></tr>
<tr><td>

Literacy Skill: Writing
Lesson Duration: 50 minutes
Link to Common Core State Standards
- **CCSS.ELA-Literacy.W.9–10.2** Write informative/explanatory texts to examine and convey complex ideas, concepts, and information clearly and accurately through the effective selection, organization, and analysis of content.
- **CCSS.ELA-Literacy.W.9–10.2b** Develop the topic with well-chosen, relevant, and sufficient facts, extended definitions, concrete details, quotations, or other information and examples appropriate to the audience's knowledge of the topic.
- **CCSS.ELA-Literacy.W.9–10.10** Write routinely over extended time frames (time for research, reflection, and revision) and shorter time frames (a single sitting or a day or two) for a range of tasks, purposes, and audiences.

</td></tr>
</table>

Learning Outcomes

As a result of this training, faculty will be able to:

- Implement the writing literacy skills: to take notes, to generate a response to what one has read, viewed, or heard, and to convey one's thinking in complete sentences.
- Use a foldable to demonstrate understanding of a concept and organization of information.
- Instruct their students in how to use foldables to take notes.
- Instruct their students in how to complete quick writes.
- Demonstrate understanding of and use a quick write in order to increase students' retention of a concept.
- Use quick writes as a tool for checking students understanding of a topic.

I. Introduction

Welcome! Today's faculty meeting is a follow-up to the presentation by International Center consultant Lin Kuzmich during which we learned about many strategies that can help us teach students how to remember information. We have decided to focus on two strategies today that are simple, yet effective: graphic organizers/foldables and quickwrites.

During our time together today you will create a foldable and take notes with it to demonstrate understanding of a quickwrite. In addition, you will have the chance to respond to a quickwrite prompt and discuss ways this strategy could be used in your classroom.

II. Teaching the Strategy

You may remember from the previous presentation by Lin Kuzmich that the best worksheet is a blank piece of paper. Can someone explain that statement? (Answer: Having students create their own graphic organizer on blank paper rather than providing it increases the level of thinking.) *You have already been given two examples of foldables in ICLE's presentation, and many of you have already used those suggestions. Today we would like to share another.*

Please take the blank piece of paper that you have been given.

Demonstrate as you are doing this.
- *Please hold the paper horizontally and fold it in half.*
- *Take the top half of the horizontal fold and fold it back to the left.*
- *Turn the paper over and take what is now the top half of the horizontal fold and fold it back to the right.*
- *You should have an accordion foldable.*

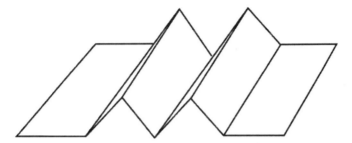

Point to the correct locations on the accordion as you give the following directions.
1. *On the top quarter with the edge facing to the left, write, "What is a quickwrite?"*
2. *Open the accordion so that the center fold is facing you.*
3. *On the left side write, "How can I use a quickwrite?"*
4. *On the right side write, "What are the benefits of a quickwrite?"*

As we work through the next section, use your foldable to take notes in the corresponding section that aligns with each question.

III. Modeling the Strategy

"Writing is to thinking fluency as phonics is to reading fluency" is a saying used by ICLE consultant Lin Kuzmich to describe how crucial writing is to student thinking and learning. When students engage in writing, they use multiple parts of their brain simultaneously and performance increase. This writing serves as a multi-sensory rehearsal for the brain and is highly correlated to increased performance on assessments. So what does this really mean to us as educators?

Writing enhances student learning in many ways. In fact, effective performance assessment demands it. While some may worry that more writing may reduce the amount of curriculum or standard coverage, studies have shown that writing does not hurt multiple-choice scores.

Let's review some data that shows how test performance increased in social science, math, and science when writing was used as a regular part of the curriculum.

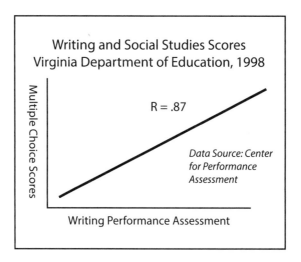

Writing and Social Studies Scores
Virginia Department of Education, 1998

R = .87

Data Source: Center for Performance Assessment

Multiple Choice Scores

Writing Performance Assessment

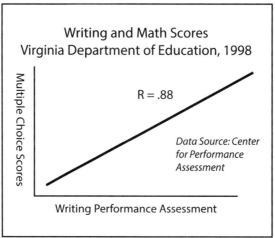

Writing and Math Scores
Virginia Department of Education, 1998

R = .88

Data Source: Center for Performance Assessment

Multiple Choice Scores

Writing Performance Assessment

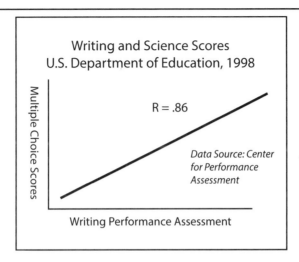

This data clearly shows the power of writing to learn. Let's look at one way you can implement more writing into your classroom.

Quickwrites are written responses to a prompt which take one to three minutes and are a few sentences in length. As they are not graded, teachers can use them as formative assessments to check for understanding, adjust pacing and emphasis, and offer assistance to those who need additional help or extension of learning.

Now, please take 30 seconds to share the notes you have taken on your foldable with the person sitting next to you.

Now that you know more about the quickwrite, let's practice using it. Pretend that you have just had a class on global warming. As a formative assessment, respond to the following prompt:

> Prompt: Define global warming and explain three factors
> that contribute to it.

Give teachers one to three minutes to respond to the quickwrite prompt. Collect the responses following the given time.

Data shows that quickwrites have proven to be most effective when used daily but not less than three times a week. They can be informal, quick, and effective formative assessments.

For example, in the quickwrite that you just completed, you responded to a question that required you to demonstrate your understanding of the day's lesson. Next I would take your responses and divide them into three piles. The first pile would be students who GOT IT. The second pile would be students who GOT SOME OF IT, and the third pile would be students who DID NOT GET IT. These quickwrites should <u>not</u> be graded; however, you can use them to address your students' individual needs in several ways.

IV. Assessment

The next day I'd break students into groups according to the piles I had made. I'd give each group a different activity to help them review the concept from the previous day. Students who "Got It" could be asked to apply the concept with a higher level of thinking. Students who "Got Some of It" could be asked to focus on areas that were missed, and those who "Did Not Get It" could be given an activity that would help them come to an understanding of the concept. I might even work closely with the last group. All this could happen in a very short amount of time, taking ten minutes or less of a class.

Now, please take 30 seconds to share your notes on how quickwrites can be used with a partner.

Hopefully you have some helpful ideas on how quickwrites can be used. Writing is an incredibly powerful tool in the learning process and helps students become more successful and more independent. Using a quickwrite can help both teachers and students: the students show what they know and give the teacher fast assessment information. This quick strategy provides incredibly powerful information.

Again, take 30 seconds to share your notes on the benefits of quickwrites with your partner.

V. Summary

Now that we have discussed the benefits of quickwrites, go to the last side of your accordion, making sure the edge of the paper is facing right.

Demonstrate the location as needed.

On that side write, "How might I use quickwrites in my classes?"

Please respond to this last question and bring your accordion foldable to your next department meeting. Your department heads will follow up with some specific instructions for the next faculty meeting; they will involve using both quickwrites and foldables in your classes during the next two weeks.

Literacy Skill: Speaking

No Opt Out and Everybody Writes

Overview

This literacy workshop was created to increase teachers' instructional effectiveness and support our efforts to improve students' speaking skills. Classroom observations indicated that many students, particularly students with disabilities and English language learners, were reluctant to participate in class discussions and would choose to remain silent. This training script provides detailed descriptions and examples of two techniques for student engagement and participation. Faculty will engage in discussions about the use of these techniques and role-play to practice implementing them in their classrooms. Using these strategies, faculty can build discussions in which all students participate and learn. These are strategies that can and should be used in every content area to encourage and promote student participation.

Faculty Training Script

No Opt Out and Everybody Writes

Literacy Skill: Writing
Lesson Duration: 50 minutes
Link to Common Core State Standards:
- **CCSS.ELA-Literacy.CCRA.R.1** Read closely to determine what the text says explicitly and to make logical inferences from it; cite specific textual evidence when writing or speaking to support conclusions drawn from the text.
- **CCSS.ELA-Literacy.W.9–10.1** Write arguments to support claims in an analysis of substantive topics or texts, using valid reasoning and relevant and sufficient evidence.

Learning Outcomes

As a result of this training, faculty will be able to:

- Implement the speaking literacy skills: to convey one's thinking in complete sentences; to participate in a class discussion or a public forum; to make an oral presentation to one's class, one's peers, or one's community; to communicate in a manner that allows one to be both heard and understood.
- Implement the writing literacy skills: to explain one's thinking; to convey one's thinking in complete sentences.
- Actively read and discuss effective instructional techniques to use school wide.
- Engage all students in classroom participation and active thinking.
- Use all these writing and discussion strategies in classes whenever appropriate.

I. Introduction

While training to be a teacher, you probably heard that you need a number of tools in your toolbox to deal with different types of students and their needs. Today we hope to add a few new tools to enhance your instruction. We need to actively seek out new ways of teaching and refine our craft for students with unexpected needs. We're going to reference the book Teaching Like a Champion by Doug Lemov and Norman Atkins for techniques you can use regularly to enhance student achievement.

Let's begin by reading pages 4–5 titled "How to Use this Book." Please actively read and think about techniques you currently use effectively. Also consider areas that you want to continue to develop.

Pages 4–5 of *Teaching Like a Champion* deal with the design of the book: you can pick what you want to focus on or read the book cover to cover. This section stresses that although you may be familiar with a technique, you can continue to improve. The section also suggests that improving on your strengths may have a more immediate effect than focusing on weaknesses.

Based on the conditions described in pages 4–5, we chose techniques that

- *can be incorporated into classrooms, school wide,*
- *"operate in synergy" with our existing literacy strategies, and*
- *may take what is already being done well to the next level.*

II. Teaching the Strategy

Technique #1: No Opt Out

What do you do when a student doesn't know the answer or does not want to answer a question? **Ask for volunteers to share some examples.**

Take a few minutes to actively read pages 27–34 of Teach Like a Champion. As you're reading, please frame your thinking around the following discussion questions for a Think-Write-Share activity after the reading.

Discussion Questions (Think-Write-Share):
1. *What were the most important points you pulled from this section?*
2. *Of the four formats on pages 32–33, which would you most likely use in your classroom?*
3. *Describe the No-Opt-Out strategies you already use.*

Summary of No Opt Out—Use the following during the Share portion of the activity to fill in any gaps in participants' understanding.
- *"It is not okay not to try."*
- *Begin with high expectations for all students all the time.*
- *Ensure that all students take responsibility for learning.*
- *Establish a tone of student accountability.*
- *"I don't know" is the Rosetta stone of work avoidance.*
- *"The sequence that begins with a student unable to answer a question should end with the student answering that question as often as possible."*
- *Allow for rehearsed success: get it wrong, and then get it right.*

Technique #2: Everybody Writes

As you think about other ways to ensure that no student "opts out," remember the previous statement at our trainings that writing is thinking. If you can get students writing, they will demonstrate their thinking process and actively participate. With this in mind, let's actively read pages 137–141 about the strategy titled "Everybody Writes." As you read, think about the ways you currently use writing in your class and how this new strategy can prevent students from opting out. We'll debrief this reading through a Think-Write-Share with the following discussion questions.

Discussion Questions (Think-Write-Share):
  1. *What were the most important points you pulled from this section?*
  2. *Share some Everybody Writes techniques that you use in your classes.*
  3. *How can Everybody Writes link to No Opt Out?*

Summary of Everybody Writes—Use the following during the Share portion to fill in any gaps in participants' understanding.

- *Allow students to prepare for more ambitious thinking/discussion by writing first.*

> *I write to know what I think.*
> *—Joan Didion*

- *As an entry ticket into class or prior to a discussion, have students respond to a prompt by first writing out their ideas and questions. When the discussion begins, everyone has something to contribute.*

Some benefits include:
- *You can select effective responses as you've already reviewed their ideas.*
- *You can more easily cold call on students since you know everyone is prepared.*
- *Every student has an opportunity to be part of the conversation.*
- *Having students write helps them process and refine their thoughts, improving the quality of their ideas and overall writing.*
- *You set a standard or steer the direction.*
- *Students remember twice as much if they write it down.*

III. Modeling the Strategy

Our challenge today is determining how you will put these techniques into practice. Using consistent language across classrooms and across the school is essential to students understanding that everyone is held to the same high expectations; regardless of the class, there is no opt out. Working with your table group, review the four No-Opt-Out formats on pages 32–33, and discuss which ones would work best in your classroom. Following the discussion, take turns at your table group practicing the No-Opt-Out procedures using a content area question. The question does not have to be particularly rigorous for your colleagues; this exercise is more about practicing how you will ensure that they answer.

You can also include Everybody Writes as a way to provide wait time and give students an opportunity to process your questions before answering.

IV. Summary

As a summary of our day, spend the last few minutes scanning through Teach Like a Champion and choosing two techniques that you would be willing to lead a discussion about in an interdisciplinary group. Please write your choices on a piece of paper, and hand them to me as you leave. As you go back into your classroom, please be consistent with your language: in our school no one can opt out and everybody writes.

Literacy Skills:
Reasoning and Reading
Reading Visuals and Active Reading

Overview

This training script focuses on developing students' skills in reading and analyzing visuals that appear on the MCAS, the SAT, ACT, and are used in teachers' assessments in all content areas. The Restructuring Committee noted that there were many questions on state assessments and the SAT that incorporated complicated webs, flow charts, graphs, and other visuals, particularly in math and science. A review of our students' performance indicated that our students were not using the information included in the visual to help them answer the question. In this literacy workshop, teachers learn the process for helping students apply pre-reading strategies to visuals, and then incorporate a five step process to work through the visual prior to answering the question. Essentially this process provides the students with a thinking routine. These strategies align to the Common Core State Standards below and focus on students improving their reading and reasoning skills. While students may have some experience reading visuals, this session helps them make predictions, interpret and evaluate content, and generate a response. These skills are most valuable as they transcend all grade levels and content areas.

Faculty Training Script

Reading Visuals and Active Reading

Literacy Skills: Reasoning and Reading
Lesson Duration: 50 minutes
Link to Common Core State Standards
- **CCSS.ELA-Literacy.CCRA.R.7** Integrate and evaluate content presented in diverse media and formats, including visually and quantitatively, as well as in words.
- **CCSS.ELA-Literacy.Reading for Sci/Tech.7** Translate quantitative or technical information expressed in words in a text into visual form (e.g., a table or chart) and translate information expressed visually or mathematically (e.g., in an equation) into words.

Learning Outcomes:
As a result of this training, faculty will be able to:
- Implement the reasoning skills: to create, interpret, and explain a table, chart, or graph; to read, breakdown, and solve a word problem; to identify a pattern, explain a pattern, and/or make a prediction based on a pattern; to explain the logic of an argument or a solution.
- Implement the reading skill: to understand a concept and construct meaning.
- Model the five steps for reading and analyzing a visual for their students.
- Instruct their students in the reading and analyzing visuals process using guided practice and independent practice.
- Apply the five steps of reading and analyzing visuals to their content area.
- Interpret and evaluate content as it relates to the visuals used.

I. Introduction

Have the following Everybody Writes prompt displayed—"When you ask students to actively read, what do they do?"—as participants come into the room: Make a prediction about the connections between reading visuals and active reading of direction, prompts, and questions.

Welcome to Reading Visuals and Active Reading. As you come in today, find your color group and begin the Everybody Writes prompt posted on the board. **Give participants time to answer the prompt. This individual opening activity will not be discussed.**

Our goal in this session is to combine strategies to create a process that will help students:
- *Reason to make predictions*
- *Explain and interpret relationships*
- *Apply pre-reading strategies*
- *Generate a written a response*
- *Convey thinking through speaking*

Before we begin, let's review our agenda. We started with the Everybody Writes prompt. Next we'll review reading visuals and connect today's topic to literacy strategies. We'll follow that up with some group work time and discussion and close the day with another Everybody Writes. Are there any questions before we begin?

II. Teaching the Strategy

We will revisit the five steps for Reading Visuals and connect the last step to the Active Reading Questions Analysis strategies we have worked on in previous meetings.

The inherent connection between Reading Visuals and Active Reading is like two puzzle pieces. The fifth step—analyze the question—is what you do in Active Reading when you deconstruct the question, prompts, and directions.

We know that when students consistently apply Reading Visuals and Active Reading strategies, they perform better on class assignments and standardized assessments; more importantly, they are better prepared for college and career endeavors. On the MCAS math and science tests, the questions often begin with basic recall. Questions follow that build on this knowledge, and the final question often requires higher order thinking skills such as synthesis, justification, or evaluation.

*The process of reading a visual begins with understanding and analyzing the given information **before** attempting to answer the questions or solve a problem. Let's look at the following example together. With each visual you read, look at five main areas:*

- *Introductory information sets the stage and gives any necessary background information.*
- *Title may provide more context or a short synopsis of what is covered.*
- *Key or legend helps you understand the visual.*
- *Labels and parenthetical information also provide additional context and help with understanding the visual.*
- *Correlations provide any additional connections the reader may need.*

Introductory information	The graph below shows changes in the birth rate and death rate for a large population of deer over a 20-year study period.
Title	
Key or Legend	
Labels and parenthetical information	
Correlations	

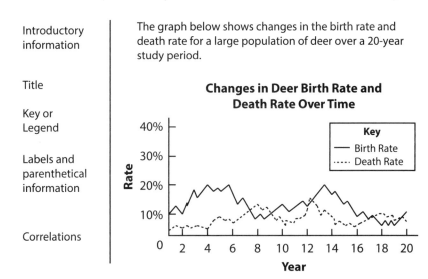

Changes in Deer Birth Rate and Death Rate Over Time

Let's review the five steps of reading a visual:
- *Identify the type of visual: is it a chart, graph, or image?*
- *Determine the topic of the visual: what is the overall theme and focus?*
- *Examine the given information from the visual: focus on all the visuals and text available, even introductory information.*
- *Develop predictions, deductions, inferences, or conclusions about the visual: start to formulate an opinion on what is happening in the visuals and what it means.*
- *Analyze the questions being asked and determine what information is needed from the visuals: narrow down what is important information to answer the question and what may be unnecessary information.*

III. Modeling the Strategy

Let's take some time to practice and see what this looks like using the following question:

17. *Carla collects employment data. At the end of 2005, she asked a group of 24 employees at Company P how many years each had worked at that company. She asked the same question of a group of 24 employees at Company Q. The line plots below show her results, where each X represents one employee.*

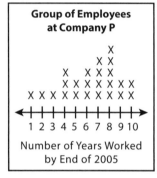

Group of Employees at Company P

Number of Years Worked by End of 2005

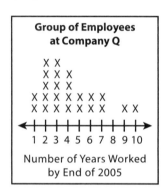

Group of Employees at Company Q

Number of Years Worked by End of 2005

Starting with the steps we've previously identified, make some possible student predictions about what the visual is and what the visual is trying to convey to us:

Possible responses: Participants may identify the visual as a plot, a line plot, or a frequency plot/table. The visual clearly identifies the number of years each employee has worked at company P or Q. The given information is the number of years each employee has worked through the end of 2005 and the total number of employees.

Possible predictions: The employees at company P have worked there longer than the employees at company Q. The workforce at company P is probably more experienced. Participants may anticipate reasons such as the pay or working conditions are better at company P. They may think more people have recently retired from company Q.

You've made some valid predications based on the data. I think they are certainly in line with what students would say.

Let's think back to the fifth step of Reading Visuals and consider how it connects to active reading, specifically question analysis. In other words, step 5 of Reading Visuals is the active reading of directions, prompts, or questions. Good readers use active reading of questions, prompts, and directions to determine the PURPOSE of the reading assignment or task.

Remember the four steps of active reading—read the question, circle key words and underline important information, paraphrase the question, and develop your plan. Let's go back to our original example and use the first three steps of active reading question analysis. Model the process for participants.

17. Carla collects employment data. At the end of 2005, she asked a group of 24 employees at Company P how many years each had worked at that company. She asked the same question of a group of 24 employees at Company Q. The line plots below show her results, where each X represents one employee.

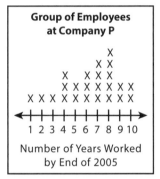

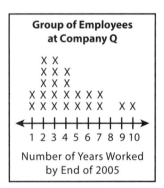

a. For the group of employees at <u>Company P</u>, what are the following <u>measures</u> for the <u>number of years worked</u> by the end of 2005?

- (mode)
- (median)

(Show) or (explain) how you got each of <u>your answers</u>.

Restated—I need to find the mode (the number that appears most) and the median (the number that represents the middle) for Company P and explain my answer.

We circled the important key words mode, median, show, *and* explain; *we underlined important information such as* Company P, measures, number of years worked, *and* your answers. *Look at how we rephrased the question. Does anyone have any questions about what we've done here?* **Answer questions as necessary.**

Now let's look at Part B. How would you apply the Active Reading: Question Analysis steps to this question?

17. *Carla collects employment data. At the end of 2005, she asked a group of 24 employees at Company P how many years each had worked at that company. She asked the same question of a group of 24 employees at Company Q. The line plots below show her results, where each X represents one employee.*

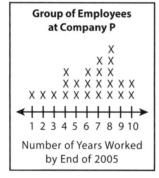
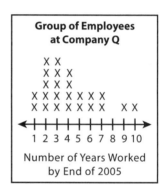

b. For the group of employees at Company Q, what are the following measures for the number of years worked by the end of 2005?

- mode
- median

Show or explain how you got each of your answers.

Do not give time for them to write this down. The question is asking the same thing for Company Q that Part A asked for Company P. Point out that the active reading steps 1–3 should look the same for this question.

Lastly, let's look at Part C of this question: I've demonstrated here the completed Active Reading Question Analysis Steps 1–3 for Part C. Does anyone have a question about this process so far? **Answer questions as necessary.**

17. *Carla collects employment data. At the end of 2005, she asked a group of 24 employees at Company P how many years each had worked at that company. She asked the same question of a group of 24 employees at Company Q. The line plots below show her results, where each X represents one employee.*

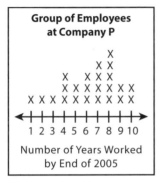

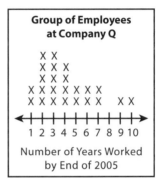

c. <u>Without computing the mean</u> for either group, ⟨use⟩ the <u>line plots</u> to ⟨determine⟩ which group of employees has the <u>greater mean number of years worked</u> by the end of 2005. ⟨Explain⟩ <u>how you got your answer</u> without computing the means.

Restated: Without calculating, find the company with the higher average number of years worked. Explain how I found the answer.

The final step in the Active Reading: Question Analysis process is to create a plan. This requires students to reason through the process they will use to answer the questions. The plan does not have to have a specific look or style to it. However, in the beginning, you may wish to provide a template for this step to help your students figure out how to create a plan.

IV. Assessment

Now it's time to practice the skills we want students to use. When I finish the instructions, move to the visual of the number that appears on your sticky note. With your group, apply the Reading Visuals and Active Reading strategies to the visual and questions. This process does NOT require you to solve the problems. You will have eight minutes to work with your group. Then return to your original table and complete the Everybody Writes.

After 8 minutes: *If you haven't done so already, return to your table and complete the Everybody Writes prompt—a reflection on what this activity will look like in your classes. This is an individual activity. You have three minutes to complete it.*

At your tables, discuss how the Reading Visuals process can benefit students and what the combined strategies will look like in your classes. Someone from each group will report out to the whole class a summary of your discussion.

Ask for volunteers from each group to share out a summary. Ensure that everyone in the group reached a consensus.

Your Turn
Move to your number groups. Apply the Reading Visuals and Active Reading strategies to your assigned question. Return to your color groups. Everybody Writes—a reflection on what this activity (the reading visuals and active reading process) will look like in your classes. Discuss with the people at your table. Someone from each color group will summarize the small group discussion for the whole group.

V. Summary

At the beginning of this workshop, you were asked to make a prediction about the connection between the two strategies. Briefly review your prediction and then complete the following closer:

- *How close was your prediction about the connections between the two strategies?*
- *In what ways has this workshop helped you prepare to use both strategies together in the upcoming weeks?*

We know these strategies work alone but are far more effective together. Please continuously use these strategies in your instruction. When we are consistent, they are successful.